Presented to:

....

From:

....

Date:

....

A CHARLES DICKENS DEVOTIONAL

COMPILED *and* WRITTEN *by*
JEAN FISCHER

A Division of Thomas Nelson Publishers

THOMAS NELSON
Since 1798

NASHVILLE   DALLAS   MEXICO CITY   RIO DE JANEIRO

A Charles Dickens Devotional

© 2012 by Thomas Nelson®, Inc.

Published in Nashville, Tennessee, by Thomas Nelson®. Thomas Nelson is a registered trademark of Thomas Nelson, Inc.

Created by MacKenzie Howard.
Cover design by Greg Jackson, Thinkpen Graphic Design.
Page design by Lori Lynch.
Project managed by Michelle Prater Burke.

Thomas Nelson, Inc., titles may be purchased in bulk for educational, business, fund-raising, or sales promotional use. For information, please e-mail SpecialMarkets@ ThomasNelson.com.

ISBN 978-1-4003-1954-1

Printed in China

12 13 14 15 RRD 6 5 4 3 2 1

www.thomasnelson.com

THERE IS A WISDOM OF THE HEAD,
AND . . . THERE IS A WISDOM
OF THE HEART.

—Charles Dickens, *Hard Times*

TABLE OF CONTENTS

Introduction

INTRODUCTION

*C*harles Dickens is considered by many to be the grand master of Victorian English literature. Well known for his vibrant characters and themes of social injustice and moral decline, Dickens's writing has weathered a sea of cultural changes in the nearly two hundred years since early publication. In that time, his novels have delighted many generations of readers.

With protagonists overcoming vain and worldly obstacles and villains who act outside the realm of Christian values, Dickens's stories teach readers life lessons richly inlaid with the fruits of the Spirit—love, joy, peace, longsuffering, kindness, goodness, and faithfulness.

Hidden like gems among the pages of his novels are numerous religious images and biblical references: in *Great Expectations*, Pip praying for the Lord to be merciful to Abel Magwitch, a sinner and formidable criminal; in *Bleak House*, the image of Christ "stooped down, writing with his finger in the dust when they brought the sinful woman to him"; in *Little Dorrit*, adoration of wealth described as "the camel in the needle's eye."

The goal of this devotional is to connect you with the spirit of Christ through the words of Charles Dickens. The influence of Dickens's faith on his work is evident in a letter he wrote in 1870 (the same year he died): "I have always striven in my writings to express veneration for the life and lessons of our Saviour—*because I feel it.*"

For each devotional entry, take a few moments to reflect,

ponder, and allow the Dickensian excerpt and corresponding devotional to shape your thinking and influence your character. May this book award you a greater connection to the "life and lessons of our Saviour," and may you "feel it" just as Dickens did.

In his final hours, Charles Dickens's thoughts were on Christ and eternity: "A brilliant morning shines on the old city," he wrote on his deathbed. "Its antiquities and ruins are surpassingly beautiful . . . Changes of glorious light from moving boughs, songs of birds, scents from gardens, woods, and fields . . . penetrate into the Cathedral, subdue its earthy odour, and preach the Resurrection and the Life."

As you read *A Charles Dickens Devotional*, may your heart also turn toward Christ our Savior, the Resurrection and the Life.

MORNING!

That punctual servant of all work, the sun, had just risen, and begun to strike a light on the morning of the thirteenth of May, one thousand eight hundred and twenty-seven, when Mr. Samuel Pickwick burst like another sun from his slumbers, threw open his chamber window, and looked out upon the world beneath. Goswell Street was at his feet, Goswell Street was on his right hand—as far as the eye could reach, Goswell Street extended on his left; and the opposite side of Goswell Street was over the way. "Such," thought Mr. Pickwick, "are the narrow views of those philosophers who, content with examining the things that lie before them, look not to the truths which are hidden beyond. As well might I be content to gaze on Goswell Street for ever, without one effort to penetrate to the hidden countries which on every side surround it." And having given vent to this beautiful reflection, Mr. Pickwick proceeded to put himself into his clothes, and his clothes into his portmanteau. Great men are seldom over scrupulous in the arrangement of their attire; the operation of shaving, dressing, and coffee-imbibing was soon performed; and, in another hour, Mr. Pickwick, with his portmanteau in his hand, his telescope in his great-coat pocket, and his note-book in his waistcoat, ready for the reception of any discoveries worthy of being noted down, had arrived at the coach-stand in St. Martin's-le-Grand. "Cab!" said Mr. Pickwick.

—The Pickwick Papers

*S*amuel Pickwick, a retired businessman, met the new day with enthusiasm. He saw it with the potential of discovery and maybe even adventure. If Pickwick and his friends from the Pickwick Club loved anything at all, it was searching for adventure. Every morning held the prospect of something new, something exciting.

How should we meet each new day? Psalm 118:24 tells us, "This is the day the LORD has made; we will rejoice and be glad in it." We should greet each day expecting God's kindness: "Through the LORD's mercies we are not consumed, because His compassions fail not. They are new every morning" (Lamentations 3:22–23). We should pray in the morning: "But to You I have cried out, O LORD, and in the morning my prayer comes before You" (Psalm 88:13). And we should view morning as a pleasant, sweet time: "Truly the light is sweet, and it is pleasant for the eyes to behold the sun" (Ecclesiastes 11:7).

When you arise in the morning, do you throw open the window and look out at the world? Do you observe the same old things, or do you notice subtle changes, like buds opening on flowers, the scent of lilacs on the breeze, or the new song of a distant bird? This is the day the Lord has made! Rejoice in His bountiful, beautiful gift.

✣

THAT THEY MAY KNOW FROM THE RISING OF THE
SUN TO ITS SETTING
THAT THERE IS NONE BESIDES ME.
I AM THE LORD, AND THERE IS NO OTHER.

Isaiah 45:6

GOD'S VOICE

A few days have elapsed, and a stately ship is out at sea, spreading its white wings to the favouring wind.

Upon the deck, image to the roughest man on board of something that is graceful, beautiful, and harmless—something that it is good and pleasant to have there, and that should make the voyage prosperous—is Florence. It is night, and she and Walter sit alone, watching the solemn path of light upon the sea between them and the moon.

At length she cannot see it plainly, for the tears that fill her eyes; and then she lays her head down on his breast, and puts her arms around his neck, saying, "Oh Walter, dearest love, I am so happy!"

Her husband holds her to his heart, and they are very quiet, and the stately ship goes on serenely.

"As I hear the sea," says Florence, "and sit watching it, it brings so many days into my mind. It makes me think so much—"

"Of Paul, my love. I know it does."

Of Paul and Walter. And the voices in the waves are always whispering to Florence, in their ceaseless murmuring, of love—of love, eternal and illimitable, not bounded by the confines of this world, or by the end of time, but ranging still, beyond the sea, beyond the sky, to the invisible country far away!

—Dombey and Son

ickens's love scenes are often wrought with emotion. This one follows Florence Dombey's wedding to Walter Gay. In the last paragraph, Dickens writes about voices in the waves whispering to Florence. He describes them as reaching beyond this world, beyond the sky "to the invisible country far away." Perhaps when Dickens wrote this, he imagined the voice of God.

In the New King James Version, God's voice is described as "a still small voice" (1 Kings 19:12). The New International Version translates this as "a gentle whisper." In modern times we might recognize this whispering in our hearts as a conscience—the small voice inside us that leads us in the right way. Isaiah 30:21 says, "Your ears shall hear a word behind you, saying, 'This is the way, walk in it.'" And in Hebrews 4:12 we discover that "the word of God is living and powerful, and sharper than any two-edged sword, piercing even to the division of soul and spirit, and of joints and marrow, and is a discerner of the thoughts and intents of the heart."

When we hear our "conscience" speak to us, we should be careful to make certain that it is indeed God's voice that we hear. God's Word and prayer will help us to do this. God's voice will never lead us astray, nor will it contradict anything in the Bible. Thus, the more time we spend intimately with the Lord in prayer and in quiet contemplation of His Word, the better we are able to recognize His voice when He speaks.

☙

"MY SHEEP HEAR MY VOICE, AND I KNOW THEM,
AND THEY FOLLOW ME."

John 10:27

 5

THE EARTH

You may seek in vain, now, for the spot on which these sisters lived, for their very names have passed away, and dusty antiquaries tell of them as of a fable. But they dwelt in an old wooden house—old even in those days—with overhanging gables and balconies of rudely-carved oak, which stood within a pleasant orchard, and was surrounded by a rough stone wall, whence a stout archer might have winged an arrow to St. Mary's Abbey. The old abbey flourished then; and the five sisters, living on its fair domains, paid yearly dues to the black monks of St. Benedict, to which fraternity it belonged.

It was a bright and sunny morning in the pleasant time of summer, when one of those black monks emerged from the abbey portal, and bent his steps towards the house of the fair sisters. Heaven above was blue, and earth beneath was green; the river glistened like a path of diamonds in the sun; the birds poured forth their songs from the shady trees; the lark soared high above the waving corn; and the deep buzz of insects filled the air. Everything looked gay and smiling; but the holy man walked gloomily on, with his eyes bent upon the ground. The beauty of the earth is but a breath, and man is but a shadow. . . .

With eyes bent upon the ground, then, or only raised enough to prevent his stumbling over such obstacles as lay in his way, the religious man moved slowly forward.

—The Life and Adventures of Nicholas Nickleby

harles Dickens is remembered for using descriptive language to create vivid images in his readers' minds. Here, Dickens presents a vibrant picture contrasting the monk's gloomy attitude with the beauty of earth. How often do we humans walk like this monk with eyes bent to the ground, oblivious to God's magnificent creation?

Genesis 1 describes how God commanded the earth into existence. He said, "Let the water under the sky be gathered to one place, and let dry ground appear. . . . Let the land produce vegetation: seed-bearing plants and trees. . . . Let there be lights in the expanse of the sky to separate the day from the night" (vv. 9, 11, 14 NIV). When God saw what He had done, He proclaimed it good.

Earth does not belong to us; it belongs to God. Psalm 24:1 reminds us, "The earth is the LORD's, and all its fullness, the world and those who dwell therein." Our appreciation of its natural beauty is a reflection of the Spirit of God that dwells in our hearts. The Bible says that when God created man and woman, He put them on earth to work it and care for it (Genesis 2:15). We are the earth's stewards. As you care for the earth around you, take time to notice the beauty of creation and to praise its Creator.

✣

ALL THINGS WERE MADE THROUGH HIM, AND WITHOUT
HIM NOTHING WAS MADE THAT WAS MADE.

John 1:3

Concerning the Poor

The room in which the boys were fed, was a large stone hall, with a copper at one end: out of which the master, dressed in an apron . . . and assisted by one or two women, ladled the gruel at mealtimes. Of this festive composition each boy had one porringer, and no more—except on occasions of great public rejoicing, when he had two ounces and a quarter of bread besides.

The bowls never wanted washing. The boys polished them with their spoons till they shone again; and when they had performed this operation . . . they would sit staring at the copper, with such eager eyes, as if they could have devoured the very bricks of which it was composed . . . Oliver Twist . . . was desperate with hunger, and reckless with misery. He rose from the table; and advancing to the master, basin and spoon in hand, said: . . .

"Please, sir, I want some more."

The master was a fat, healthy man; but he turned very pale. He gazed in stupefied astonishment on the small rebel for some seconds, and then clung for support to the copper. The assistants were paralysed with wonder; the boys with fear.

"What!" said the master at length, in a faint voice.

"Please, sir," replied Oliver, "I want some more."

The master aimed a blow at Oliver's head with the ladle; pinioned him in his arm; and shrieked aloud for the beadle.

—Oliver Twist

In this scene, Oliver and the other boys in Mr. Bumble's workhouse are near starvation after working hard and having very little to eat. The boys allotted Oliver the task of asking for more food, something for which he surely will be punished. Many of Dickens's works, particularly *Oliver Twist*, reflect his sympathy for the poor and his distain for aristocratic heartlessness.

In the Bible, God commanded Moses to have a right attitude toward the poor. He said, "The poor will never cease from the land; therefore I command you, saying, 'You shall open your hand wide to your brother, to your poor and your needy, in your land'" (Deuteronomy 15:11). The Bible promises God's favor when we give to the poor: "If you extend your soul to the hungry and satisfy the afflicted soul, then your light shall dawn in the darkness, and your darkness shall be as the noonday. The LORD will guide you continually, and satisfy your soul in drought, and strengthen your bones; you shall be like a watered garden, and like a spring of water, whose waters do not fail" (Isaiah 58:10–11).

The favor that God shows us when we give to the poor is the satisfaction that we have done His will. We can help many people like Oliver by allowing God to lead us to the ways in which He wants us to help. Consider, today, how God may be leading you.

✣

OPEN YOUR MOUTH, JUDGE RIGHTEOUSLY,
AND PLEAD THE CAUSE OF THE POOR AND NEEDY.

Proverbs 31:9

ABOUT GRUMBLING

"A merry Christmas, uncle! God save you!" cried a cheerful voice. It was the voice of Scrooge's nephew, who came upon him so quickly that this was the first intimation he had of his approach.

"Bah!" said Scrooge, "Humbug!"

He had so heated himself with rapid walking in the fog and frost, this nephew of Scrooge's, that he was all in a glow . . .

"Christmas a humbug, uncle!" said Scrooge's nephew. "You don't mean that, I am sure?"

"I do," said Scrooge. "Merry Christmas! What right have you to be merry? What reason have you to be merry? You're poor enough."

"Come, then," returned the nephew gaily. "What right have you to be dismal? What reason have you to be morose? You're rich enough."

Scrooge having no better answer ready on the spur of the moment, said, "Bah!" again; and followed it up with "Humbug."

"Don't be cross, uncle!" said the nephew.

"What else can I be," returned the uncle, "when I live in such a world of fools as this? Merry Christmas! . . . What's Christmas time to you but a time for paying bills without money; a time for finding yourself a year older, but not an hour richer; a time for balancing your books and having every item in 'em through a round dozen of months presented dead against you? If I could work my will," said Scrooge indignantly, "every idiot who goes about with 'Merry Christmas' on his lips, should be boiled with his own pudding, and buried with a stake of holly through his heart!"

—A Christmas Carol

Ebenezer Scrooge, Dickens's most well-known character, personifies the very definition of grumpiness. He is crabby, cranky, cross, crotchety, irritable, irascible, petulant, prickly, short-tempered, snappish, snarky, snippety, stuffy, and testy too! His bad attitude separates him not only from people, but also from God.

When the Israelites wandered around the wilderness searching for the promised land, they felt grumpy, and they grumbled to their leader, Moses. "If only we had died by the LORD's hand in Egypt! There we sat around pots of meat and ate all the food we wanted, but you have brought us out into this desert to starve this entire assembly to death" (Exodus 16:3 NIV). Moses answered them, "Who are we? You are not grumbling against us, but against the LORD" (v. 8 NIV). In the New Testament, Jesus told His disciples, "Stop grumbling among yourselves" (John 6:43 NIV). And in Philippians 2:14–15 (NIV), Paul says, "Do everything without complaining or arguing, so that you may become blameless and pure, children of God without fault in a crooked and depraved generation."

Complaining focuses on our dislikes instead of our blessings. Grumbling, as Moses said, is in truth grumbling against God. If we will but turn our complaining hearts into thankful hearts, then we will discover just how blessed we are.

⚜

I WILL FORGET MY COMPLAINT, I WILL PUT OFF MY SAD
FACE AND WEAR A SMILE.

Job 9:27

ORDER FROM CHAOS

The first shock of a great earthquake had . . . rent the whole neighbour-hood to its centre. Traces of its course were visible on every side. Houses were knocked down; streets broken through and stopped; deep pits and trenches dug in the ground; enormous heaps of earth and clay thrown up; buildings that were undermined and shaking, propped by great beams of wood. Here, a chaos of carts, overthrown and jumbled together, lay topsy-turvy at the bottom of a steep unnatural hill; there, confused treasures of iron soaked and rusted in something that had accidentally become a pond. Everywhere were bridges that led nowhere; thoroughfares that were wholly impassable; Babel towers of chimneys, wanting half their height; temporary wooden houses and enclosures, in the most unlikely situations; carcases of ragged tenements, and fragments of unfinished walls and arches, and piles of scaffolding, and wildernesses of bricks, and giant forms of cranes, and tripods straddling above nothing. There were a hundred thousand shapes and substances of incompleteness, wildly mingled out of their places, upside down, burrowing in the earth, aspiring in the air, mouldering in the water, and unintelligible as any dream. . . . Boiling water hissed and heaved within dilapidated walls . . . and mounds of ashes blocked up rights of way, and wholly changed the law and custom of the neighbourhood.

In short, the yet unfinished and unopened Railroad was in progress; and, from the very core of all this dire disorder, trailed smoothly away, upon its mighty course of civilisation and improvement.

—Dombey and Son

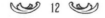

In Dickens's time, the city of London rapidly changed as the railroad was built. In an already filthy environment, there were debris and disorder as buildings came down to make way for tracks, bridges, railway stations, and new businesses to support new needs. Dickens, who often walked the streets of London, searching for scenes for his books, incorporated this shifting infrastructure into the settings of his later works, as in this passage from *Dombey and Son*. It presents an image of chaos without even a hint of order. And although we modern readers know that order did eventually come from the chaos, Dickens's contemporary readers were left to wonder what would become of London.

From the foundation of time, we find God creating order from chaos. Genesis 1 says that in the beginning the earth was without form, and God shaped it into something perfect. In 1 Corinthians 14:33, we discover that "God is not the author of confusion but of peace." He always has a plan, and He always works that plan into being (Psalm 33:11).

Look at the world today, and, like Dickens, you might see chaos. Often, it seems that things are out of control. But keep in mind that wherever chaos enters, there is hope. The familiar Bible verse Romans 8:28 says, "We know that all things work together for good to those who love God." Our heavenly Father specializes in chaotic situations. He can bring harmony where disorder reigns.

☙

"ABBA, FATHER, ALL THINGS ARE POSSIBLE FOR YOU."

Mark 14:36

THE BOOK OF PROVERBS

"Fred!" said Mr. Swiveller, finding that his former adjuration had been productive of no effect. "Pass the rosy."

Young Trent with an impatient gesture pushed the glass towards him, and fell again in the moody attitude from which he had been unwillingly roused.

"I'll give you, Fred," said his friend, stirring the mixture, "a little sentiment appropriate to the occasion. Here's May the—"

"Pshaw!" interposed the other. "You worry me to death with your chattering. You can be merry under any circumstances."

"Why, Mr. Trent," returned Dick, "there is a proverb which talks about being merry and wise. There are some people who can be merry and can't be wise, and some who can be wise (or think they can) and can't be merry. I'm one of the first sort. If the proverb's a good 'un, I suppose it's better to keep to half of it than none; at all events, I'd rather be merry and not wise, than like you, neither one nor t'other."

"Bah!" muttered his friend, peevishly.

"With all my heart," said Mr. Swiveller. "In the polite circles I believe this sort of thing isn't usually said to a gentleman in his own apartments, but never mind that. Make yourself at home," adding to this retort an observation to the effect that his friend appeared to be rather "cranky" in point of temper, Richards Swiveller finished the rosy and applied himself to the composition of another glassful, in which, after tasting it with great relish, he proposed a toast to an imaginary company.

—The Old Curiosity Shop

Read the works of Charles Dickens, and you are sure to come across many proverbs and proverbial expressions. Through his characters and descriptive prose, Dickens often offered wisdom to his readers, as he did through this dialogue between Fred Trent and Dick Swiveller.

Solomon, son of Israel's King David, wrote the book of Proverbs in the Bible. It is a book filled with wisdom about many topics. Solomon begins his book by explaining its purpose: "The proverbs of Solomon son of David, king of Israel: for gaining wisdom and instruction; for understanding words of insight; for receiving instruction in prudent behavior, doing what is right and just and fair; for giving prudence to those who are simple, knowledge and discretion to the young—let the wise listen and add to their learning, and let the discerning get guidance—for understanding proverbs and parables, the sayings and riddles of the wise" (Proverbs 1:1–6 NIV).

The Bible says that Solomon spoke three thousand proverbs, and that all the kings of the world had heard his wisdom (1 Kings 4:32, 34). God divinely inspired the book of Proverbs so that there is a proverb to speak to every part of our lives. It is a book that we can read again and again and still find new wisdom for our present circumstances. Open up the book of Proverbs and search out a bit of wisdom for yourself today.

✣

AND GOD GAVE SOLOMON WISDOM AND EXCEEDINGLY
GREAT UNDERSTANDING, AND LARGENESS OF HEART
LIKE THE SAND ON THE SEASHORE.

1 Kings 4:29

CHRISTIAN CLEANLINESS

Mrs. Joe was prodigiously busy in getting the house ready for the festivities of the day, and Joe had been put upon the kitchen doorstep to keep him out of the dust-pan . . .

Joe . . . ventured into the kitchen after me as the dustpan had retired before us . . . [He] secretly crossed his two forefingers, and exhibited them to me, as our token that Mrs. Joe was in a cross temper. . . .

We were to have a superb dinner, consisting of a leg of pickled pork and greens, and a pair of roast stuffed fowls. . . .

So, we had our slices served out, as if we were two thousand troops on a forced march instead of a man and boy at home . . . In the mean-time, Mrs. Joe put clean white curtains up, and tacked a new flowered flounce across the wide chimney to replace the old one, and uncovered the little state parlor . . . , which was never uncovered at any other time, but passed the rest of the year in a cool haze of silver paper, which even extended to the four little white crockery poodles on the mantel-shelf, each with a black nose and a basket of flowers in his mouth . . . Mrs. Joe was a very clean housekeeper, but had an exquisite art of making her cleanliness more uncomfortable and unacceptable than dirt itself. Cleanliness is next to Godliness, and some people do the same by their religion.

—*Great Expectations*

Pip, the orphaned main character of *Great Expectations* and narrator of this passage, resides with the Gargerys— Pip's abusive sister and her kind husband, Joe. Mrs. Joe keeps her house hospital clean, and heaven help anyone who dirties it! In his description, Dickens purposely fashions her home as the antithesis of Christian cleanliness.

You will not find the proverb "Cleanliness is next to godliness" in the Bible, but the Scriptures have much to say on the topic of keeping clean. The Old Testament offers scores of laws concerning cleanliness in its literal sense; however, when Jesus arrived, He had a new interpretation. In Mark 7, we read that the Pharisees criticized Jesus' disciples for eating bread with unclean hands—against the traditions of their elders (vv. 1–13). Jesus told them that "unclean" does not mean dirty hands or a dirty house, but a dirty heart (vv. 18–23). In His Sermon on the Mount, He told the crowd, "Blessed are the pure in heart, for they shall see God" (Matthew 5:8).

In a spiritual sense, cleanliness *is* next to godliness. A clean heart is our pathway to God. Christian cleanliness means being pure in our thoughts, attitudes, and in everything we do. The apostle John said, "If we confess our sins, [God] is faithful and just to forgive us our sins and to cleanse us from all unrighteousness" (1 John 1:9).

✣

CREATE IN ME A CLEAN HEART, O GOD,
AND RENEW A STEADFAST SPIRIT WITHIN ME.

Psalm 51:10

Fear and Misfortune

As I knew she would only speak in her own good time, I sat down near her, and spoke to the birds, and played with the cat . . .

"Trot," said my aunt at last, when she had finished her tea, and carefully smoothed down her dress, and wiped her lips . . . "Trot, have you got to be firm and self-reliant?"

"I hope so, aunt." . . .

"Then why, my love," said my aunt . . . , "why do you think I prefer to sit upon this property of mine tonight?"

I shook my head, unable to guess.

"Because," said my aunt, "it's all I have. Because I'm ruined, my dear!"

If the house, and every one of us, had tumbled out into the river together, I could hardly have received a greater shock. . . .

"I am ruined, my dear Trot! All I have in the world is in this room, except the cottage; and that I have left Janet to let. . . . We'll talk about this, more, tomorrow."

I was roused from my amazement, and concern for her—I am sure, for her—by her falling on my neck, for a moment, and crying that she only grieved for me. In another moment she suppressed this emotion; and said with an aspect more triumphant than dejected:

"We must meet reverses boldly, and not suffer them to frighten us, my dear. We must learn to act the play out. We must live misfortune down, Trot!"

—David Copperfield

The older characters in Dickens's novels often have wise words for the younger generation. In this conversation between young David Copperfield and his aunt, Miss Betsey Trotwood, the lesson is about meeting misfortune head-on without fear.

God does not want us to be afraid when trouble strikes. The Bible says in 2 Timothy 1:7, "For God has not given us a spirit of fear, but of power and love and of a sound mind." In Isaiah 41:10 (NASB), God says, "Do not fear, for I am with you; do not anxiously look about you, for I am your God. I will strengthen you, surely I will help you."

We can conquer fear if we first put our faith in God. Romans 10:17 tells us how to do this: "Faith comes by hearing, and hearing by the word of God." When we arm ourselves with scripture, we have weapons to fight the things that frighten us. The Bible also assures us that God will rescue us whenever we are afraid. Consider this from Isaiah 35:4 (NIV): "Say to those with fearful hearts, 'Be strong, do not fear; your God will come, he will come with vengeance; with divine retribution he will come to save you.'"

⚜

THE LORD IS MY LIGHT AND MY SALVATION;
WHOM SHALL I FEAR?
THE LORD IS THE STRENGTH OF MY LIFE;
OF WHOM SHALL I BE AFRAID?

Psalm 27:1

REST

A tranquil summer sunset shone upon him as he approached the end of his walk, and passed through the meadows by the river side. He had that sense of peace, and of being lightened of a weight of care, which country quiet awakens in the breasts of dwellers in towns. . . . The rich foliage of the trees, the luxuriant grass diversified with wild flowers, the little green islands in the river, the beds of rushes, the water-lilies floating on the surface of the stream, the distant voices in boats borne musically towards him on the ripple of the water and the evening air, were all expressive of rest. In the occasional leap of a fish, or dip of an oar, or twittering of a bird not yet at roost, or distant barking of a dog, or lowing of a cow—in all such sounds, there was the prevailing breath of rest, which seemed to encompass him in every scent that sweetened the fragrant air. The long lines of red and gold in the sky, and the glorious track of the descending sun, were all divinely calm. Upon the purple tree-tops far away, and on the green height near at hand up which the shades were slowly creeping, there was an equal hush. Between the real landscape and its shadow in the water, there was no division; both were so untroubled and clear, and, while so fraught with solemn mystery of life and death, so hopefully reassuring to the gazer's soothed heart, because so tenderly and mercifully beautiful.

—Little Dorrit

In many of his novels, Charles Dickens wrote of the English countryside as a place of beauty and rest for his characters, a stark contrast to the bustling streets of London and its areas of poverty and filth. We can all use a place, like Dickens's countryside, where our hearts can find peace and rest.

The Bible speaks well of rest. We find it mentioned first in Genesis, chapter 2: "By the seventh day God had finished the work he had been doing; so on the seventh day he rested from all his work" (v. 2 NIV). In His Ten Commandments, God ordered the people to rest: "Six days you shall labor and do all your work, but the seventh day is a Sabbath to the LORD your God. On it you shall not do any work" (Exodus 20:9–10 NIV). God even said that the land was to have a year of rest (Leviticus 25:4).

Jesus invites us to rest in Him. "Come to me," He says, "all you who labor and are heavy laden, and I will give you rest" (Matthew 11:28). Jesus' invitation is to accept His gift of salvation. For those who do, He offers the ultimate rest— eternal rest for their souls.

AND HE SAID TO THEM, "COME ASIDE BY YOURSELVES
TO A DESERTED PLACE AND REST A WHILE."

Mark 6:31

GREAT EXPECTATIONS

"My name," he said, "is Jaggers, and I am a lawyer in London. . . . I have unusual business to transact with you, and I commence by explaining that it is not of my originating. . . ."

Finding that he could not see us very well from where he sat, he got up, and threw one leg over the back of a chair and leaned upon it; thus having one foot on the seat of the chair, and one foot on the ground.

"Now, Joseph Gargery, I am the bearer of an offer to relieve you of this young fellow your apprentice. You would not object to cancel his indentures at his request and for his good? You would want nothing for so doing?"

"Lord forbid that I should want anything for not standing in Pip's way," said Joe, staring.

"Lord forbidding is pious, but not to the purpose," returned Mr. Jaggers. "The question is, Would you want anything? Do you want anything?"

"The answer is," returned Joe, sternly, "No."

I thought Mr. Jaggers glanced at Joe, as if he considered him a fool for his disinterestedness. But I was too much bewildered between breathless curiosity and surprise, to be sure of it.

"Very well," said Mr. Jaggers. "Recollect the admission you have made, and don't try to go from it presently."

"Who's a going to try?" retorted Joe. . . .

"Now, I return to this young fellow. And the communication I have got to make is, that he has Great Expectations."

—Great Expectations

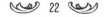

The theme of plans, hopes, and dreams runs throughout Dickens's novel *Great Expectations*. Pip came from a humble beginning, but a benefactor made it possible for him to expect to become a wealthy and educated gentleman. God was not at the center of Pip's expectations, and although Pip attained them, he found that they came with a price.

The Bible tells of a man who did put God at the center of his expectations. David expected to become king of Israel, but his expectation was hindered when King Saul promised to kill him. Instead of becoming king, David found himself running from a murderer. David wrote in one of his psalms, "My soul, wait silently for God alone, for my expectation is from Him" (Psalm 62:5). David's hope stayed firm in the Lord. He expected God to lead him in His own time and way.

When we put God at the center of our expectations, He often gives us more than we anticipate and in ways that we cannot imagine. Ephesians 3:20 says God "is able to do exceedingly abundantly above all that we ask or think." Pip's expectations led to him hurting the people he loved. He became a wealthy and educated gentleman with regrets. But because God was at the center of David's expectations, he became a great king who unified and ruled over Israel. Indeed, when our plans and dreams are rooted in God, we all can have great expectations.

⚜

A MAN'S HEART PLANS HIS WAY,
BUT THE LORD DIRECTS HIS STEPS.

Proverbs 16:9

TRUST

As Lizzie Hexam shook her head . . . and as her glance sought the fire, there was a quiet resolution in her folded hands, not lost on Bella's bright eyes.

"Have you lived much alone?" asked Bella.

"Yes. It's nothing new to me. I used to be always alone many hours together, in the day and in the night, when poor father was alive."

"You have a brother, I have been told?"

"I have a brother, but he is not friendly with me. He is a very good boy though, and has raised himself by his industry. I don't complain of him."

As she said it, with her eyes upon the fire-glow, there was an instantaneous escape of distress into her face. Bella seized the moment to touch her hand.

"Lizzie, I wish you would tell me whether you have any friend of your own sex and age."

"I have lived that lonely kind of life, that I have never had one," was the answer.

"Nor I neither," said Bella. "Not that my life has been lonely, for I could have sometimes wished it lonelier, instead of having Ma going on like the Tragic Muse with a face-ache in majestic corners, and Lavvy being spiteful—though of course I am very fond of them both. I wish you could make a friend of me, Lizzie. Do you think you could? I have no more of what they call character, my dear, than a canary-bird, but I know I am trustworthy."

—*Our Mutual Friend*

Dickens's novel *Our Mutual Friend* might never have been finished. While writing it, Dickens and his wife were in a terrible train accident that injured many and took the lives of some. Dickens, not seriously injured, climbed back into his damaged railcar to retrieve the manuscript. Otherwise, we might not know of this new friendship between two lonely girls, Bella Wilfer and Lizzie Hexam.

Bella offered herself to Lizzie as a trustworthy friend. Trust is important in any relationship, and especially in our relationship with God. In Proverbs 3:5–6, we read: "Trust in the LORD with all your heart, and lean not on your own understanding; in all your ways acknowledge Him, and He shall direct your paths." We find God directing the paths of numerous Bible heroes. In the book of Judges, Gideon—by trusting God—defeated an army of about 135,000 men with his small army of 300. Many other stories of trust are in the Bible, including Job, Noah, and Daniel, to name only a few.

Although our friends might be as trustworthy as humanly possible, God alone is worthy of perfect trust. The Bible says that God will never lie (Deuteronomy 32:4). He will not change His mind about anything He has promised us this in the Scriptures (Numbers 23:19). And He will never leave us. Jesus promises, "I am with you always, to the very end of the age" (Matthew 28:20 NIV). There can be no better friend.

✛

IN YOU, O LORD, I PUT MY TRUST.

Psalm 31:1

New Believers

This was a case of metaphysics, at least as difficult for Joe to deal with as for me. But Joe took the case altogether out of the region of metaphysics, and by that means vanquished it. . . .

"And as to being common [said Joe], I don't make it out at all clear. You are oncommon in some things [Pip]. You're oncommon small. Likewise you're a oncommon scholar."

"No, I am ignorant and backward, Joe."

"Why, see what a letter you wrote last night! Wrote in print even! I've seen letters—Ah! and from gentlefolks!—that I'll swear weren't wrote in print," said Joe.

"I have learnt next to nothing, Joe. You think much of me. It's only that."

"Well, Pip," said Joe, "be it so or be it son't, you must be a common scholar afore you can be a oncommon one, I should hope! The king upon his throne, with his crown upon his ed, can't sit and write his acts of Parliament in print, without having begun, when he were a unpromoted Prince, with the alphabet.—Ah!" added Joe, with a shake of the head that was full of meaning, "and begun at A. too, and worked his way to Z. And I know what that is to do, though I can't say I've exactly done it."

There was some hope in this piece of wisdom, and it rather encouraged me.

—Great Expectations

All learning has a starting point, as Joe Gargery points out in this conversation with his friend Pip. Even great scholars and kings began at the beginning, by learning the letter *A*. New Christians learn about God in this way too. They begin with the simple truths of the Bible, and as they grow in knowledge, they work their way through the text many times again, trying to find deeper meaning in the words.

Second Timothy 3:15 says that knowing the Holy Scriptures (the Bible) makes us wise. Psalm 119:160 tells us that all the words of the Bible are true. Hebrews 5:12 compares knowing the elementary truths of the Bible to a baby needing milk before graduating to solid food. And in Acts 15:7, the apostle Peter proclaims that the Bible should be known by all the world's people.

Where does a new Christian begin when reading the Bible? Charles Dickens wrote a book for his children called *The Life of Our Lord*. In it, he says, "The New Testament was the very best book that ever was or ever will be known in the world." The four Gospels that begin the New Testament—Matthew, Mark, Luke, and John—tell the story of Jesus' life. And what better place to continue—or begin—our Christian walk than with the One who came to save us!

☩

FOR WHATEVER THINGS WERE WRITTEN BEFORE
WERE WRITTEN FOR OUR LEARNING, THAT WE
THROUGH THE PATIENCE AND COMFORT OF THE
SCRIPTURES MIGHT HAVE HOPE.

Romans 15:4

REGARDING WORDS

"Is it possible," pursued Mr. Kenge, putting up his eye-glasses, "that our young friend . . . never heard of Jarndyce and Jarndyce!"

I shook my head, wondering even what it was.

"Not of Jarndyce and Jarndyce?" said Mr. Kenge, looking over his glasses at me and softly turning the case about and about as if he were petting something. "Not of one of the greatest Chancery suits known? Not of Jarndyce and Jarndyce—the—a—in itself a monument of Chancery practice. In which . . . every difficulty, every contingency, every masterly fiction, every form of procedure known in that court, is represented over and over again? It is a cause that could not exist, out of this free and great country. I should say that the aggregate of costs in Jarndyce and Jarndyce, . . . amounts at the present hour to from SIX-ty to SEVEN-ty THOUSAND POUNDS!" said Mr. Kenge, leaning back in his chair. . . .

He appeared to enjoy beyond everything the sound of his own voice. I couldn't wonder at that, for it was mellow and full, and gave great importance to every word he uttered. He listened to himself with obvious satisfaction and sometimes gently beat time to his own music with his head or rounded a sentence with his hand. I was very much impressed by him— even then, before I knew that he formed himself on the model of a great lord who was his client and that he was generally called Conversation Kenge.

—Bleak House

Dickens's *Bleak House* is considered by many to be his best work. It shows the perils of lengthy trials in the Courts of Chancery. One such trial is the case of Jarndyce and Jarndyce in which "Conversation Kenge" is the attorney for Mr. John Jarndyce, owner of Bleak House. Kenge's words often reflect his puffed-up self-importance.

In the Bible, the book of James has much to say on the topic of our words. James says that our tongues are restless, evil, and filled with deadly poison (3:8). He also adds that "the tongue is a small part of the body, but it makes great boasts. Consider what a great forest is set on fire by a small spark. The tongue also is a fire . . . It corrupts the whole person, sets the whole course of his life on fire . . . With the tongue we praise our Lord and Father, and with it we curse men, who have been made in God's likeness. Out of the same mouth come praise and cursing . . . This should not be" (3:5–10 NIV).

The words we speak shape our lives. The good news is that we can turn a destructive tongue into a productive one. A productive tongue knows when to speak and when not to speak. It does not gossip, swear, grumble, or complain. It speaks the truth, lifts others up, and continually praises the Lord.

⚜

LET THE WORDS OF MY MOUTH AND THE
MEDITATION OF MY HEART
BE ACCEPTABLE IN YOUR SIGHT, O LORD.

Psalm 19:14

ON PEACE

Mr. Snagsby . . . says to Mrs. Snagsby, "At what time did you expect Mr. and Mrs. Chadband, my love?"

"At six," says Mrs. Snagsby.

Mr. Snagsby observes in a mild and casual way that "it's gone that."

"Perhaps you'd like to begin without them," is Mrs. Snagsby's reproachful remark. . . .

Here, Guster . . . comes rustling . . . down the little staircase . . . and falling flushed into the drawing-room, announces that Mr. and Mrs. Chadband have appeared . . .

Mr. Chadband is a large yellow man with a fat smile and a general appearance of having a good deal of train oil in his system. Mrs. Chadband is a stern, severe-looking, silent woman. Mr. Chadband moves softly and cumbrously, not unlike a bear who has been taught to walk upright. He is very much embarrassed about the arms, as if they were inconvenient to him and he wanted to grovel, is very much in a perspiration about the head, and never speaks without first putting up his great hand, as delivering a token to his hearers that he is going to edify them.

"My friends," says Mr. Chadband, "peace be on this house! On the master thereof, on the mistress thereof, on the young maidens, and on the young men! My friends, why do I wish for peace? What is peace? Is it war? No. Is it strife? No. Is it lovely, and gentle, and beautiful, and pleasant, and serene, and joyful? Oh, yes! Therefore, my friends, I wish for peace, upon you and upon yours."

—Bleak House

harles Dickens wrote the Reverend Chadband as a hypo-critical clergyman who rarely practiced what he preached. Here, he enters the house of one of his admirers, Mrs. Snagsby, and offers a peace-filled blessing. Although his blessing may not have been sincere, Chadband's definition of peace was a good one.

What does the Bible say about peace? As Christians, we are part of one body, and we are called to peace (Colossians 3:15). We are to seek peace and pursue it (Psalm 34:14). Jesus is known as the Prince of Peace (Isaiah 9:6), and through our faith in Him, we have peace with God (Romans 5:1). God promises peace to all His people (Psalm 85:8). When we trust in Him, He will keep us in perfect peace (Isaiah 26:3). The Bible says that God's peace is so wonderful that it is beyond our understanding (Philippians 4:7).

The Bible has eleven benedictions containing the word *peace*. Unlike the Reverend Chadband's benediction in Dickens's *Bleak House*, all of the Bible's benedictions include the name of the Lord. Saint Francis of Assisi once said, "While you are proclaiming peace with your lips, be careful to have it even more fully in your heart." Let this day begin with a benediction of peace in your own heart.

✠

Now may the Lord of peace Himself give you peace always in every way. The Lord be with you all.

2 Thessalonians 3:16

CHILDHOOD INNOCENCE

"You must be tired, sir," said he as he placed a chair near the fire, "how can I thank you?"

"By taking more care of your grandchild . . . , my good friend," I replied.

"More care!" said the old man in a shrill voice, "more care of Nelly! . . ."

He said this with such evident surprise that I was perplexed what answer to make . . . "I don't think you consider—" I began.

"I don't consider!" cried the old man interrupting me, "I don't consider her! Ah, how little you know of the truth!" . . .

While we were sitting thus, . . . the door of the closet opened, and the child returned, . . . She busied herself immediately in preparing supper, and . . . I was surprised to see that . . . everything was done by the child, and that there appeared to be no other persons but ourselves in the house. I took advantage of a moment when she was absent to venture a hint on this point, to which the old man replied that there were few grown persons as trustworthy or as careful as she.

"It always grieves me," I observed, . . . "to contemplate the initiation of children into the ways of life, when they are scarcely more than infants. It checks their confidence and simplicity—two of the best qualities that Heaven gives them—and demands that they share our sorrows before they are capable of entering into our enjoyments."

—The Old Curiosity Shop

Little Nell, a child not yet fourteen years of age, was forced to grow up too soon while caring for her grandfather, the owner of the Old Curiosity Shop. Not only did she care for the old man day and night, but Nell was forced to live with him as a pauper in the streets of London after a bad debt cost the grandfather his shop. Nell's story is a sad one and a prime example of Victorian sentimentality in the literature of Dickens's time.

When we read what Dickens says about a child's confidence and simplicity being taken away too soon, we might be reminded of what Jesus said in Matthew 18:3–4: "Unless you are converted and become as little children, you will by no means enter the kingdom of heaven. Therefore whoever humbles himself as this little child is the greatest in the kingdom of heaven."

Jesus recognized the pure simplicity and innocence of a child's faith, untarnished by the issues of adulthood. He warned us against allowing our straightforward faith in God to be commandeered by the world. Has your faith been compromised by worldly demands, or is it rooted in childlike humility? Remember, it is always possible for you to approach God with the unwavering faith of a child.

✤

"I PRAISE YOU, FATHER, LORD OF HEAVEN AND
EARTH, BECAUSE YOU HAVE HIDDEN THESE THINGS
FROM THE WISE AND LEARNED, AND REVEALED THEM
TO LITTLE CHILDREN."

Luke 10:21 NIV

LIGHT OF THE WORLD

The town was glad with morning light; places that had shown ugly and distrustful all night long, now wore a smile; and sparkling sunbeams dancing on chamber windows, and twinkling through blind and curtain before sleepers' eyes, shed light even into dreams, and chased away the shadows of the night. Birds in hot rooms, covered up close and dark, felt it was morning, and chafed and grew restless in their little cells; bright-eyed mice crept back to their tiny homes and nestled timidly together; the sleek house-cat, forgetful of her prey, sat winking at the rays of sun starting through keyhole and cranny in the door, and longed for her stealthy run and warm sleek bask outside. The nobler beasts confined in dens, stood motionless behind their bars and gazed on fluttering boughs, and sunshine peeping through some little window, with eyes in which old forests gleamed—then trod impatiently the track their prisoned feet had worn—and stopped and gazed again. Men in their dungeons stretched their cramped cold limbs and cursed the stone that no bright sky could warm. The flowers that sleep by night, opened their gentle eyes and turned them to the day. The light, creation's mind, was everywhere, and all things owned its power. . . .

All was so still at that early hour, that the few pale people . . . seemed as much unsuited to the scene, as the sickly lamp which had been here and there left burning, was powerless and faint in the full glory of the sun.

—*The Old Curiosity Shop*

In this scene from *The Old Curiosity Shop*, Charles Dickens paints a vivid word picture of light for his readers. Light— one of God's first creations, or as Dickens describes it, "creation's mind."

The first verses of the Bible reveal that "in the beginning, God created the heavens and the earth. Now the earth was formless and empty, darkness was over the surface of the deep . . . And God said, 'Let there be light,' and there was light (Genesis 1:1–3 NIV). The Bible tells us that "God is light" (1 John 1:5). Perhaps the greatest scripture verse about light is John 9:5, where Jesus proclaims, "I am the light of the world." He said this because His death on the cross dispelled the darkness of our earthly sins and lit the way for our eternal life.

Sadly, there are still many people who do not know about this gift of light—Christ's gift of salvation. They walk through life in spiritual darkness. Our purpose as Christians is to bring them into the light of Christ's love. The Bible says that we should "walk as children of light," sharing Christ's gift with the world (Ephesians 5:8). You can be a light to those walking in darkness. Decide today how you will share with others Jesus' gift of eternal life.

✠

TRULY THE LIGHT IS SWEET,
AND IT IS PLEASANT FOR THE EYES TO BEHOLD THE SUN.

Ecclesiastes 11:7

ON COMMUNICATION

One day . . . I . . . told them that nothing vanished from the eye of God, though much might pass away from the eyes of men. "We were all of us," says I, "children once; and our baby feet have strolled in green woods ashore; and our baby hands have gathered flowers in gardens, where the birds were singing. The children that we were, are not lost to the great knowledge of our Creator. Those innocent creatures will appear with us before Him, and plead for us. . . . The purest part of our lives will not desert us at the pass to which all of us here present are gliding. What we were then, will be as much in existence before Him, as what we are now." . . .

We were in no want of rain-water, but we had nothing else. And yet . . . I never turned my eyes upon a waking face but it tried to brighten before mine. O, what a thing it is, in a time of danger and in the presence of death, the shining of a face upon a face! I have heard it broached that orders should be given in great new ships by electric telegraph. I admire machinery . . . and am as thankful to it as any man can be for what it does for us. But it will never be a substitute for the face of a man, with his soul in it, encouraging another man to be brave and true.

—The Wreck of the Golden Mary

harles Dickens's "The Wreck of the Golden Mary" tells the story of a shipwreck. En route from England to America, the *Golden Mary* strikes an iceberg while rounding Cape Horn. She sinks, and her passengers and crew are left stranded in rowboats waiting to be rescued. The narrator of the passage above, a man named William George Ravender, remarks about the benefits of communicating face-to-face rather than by the then-modern telegraph. Had Dickens written this story today, he might well be making the comparison to any number of today's electronic devices.

With technology we have the benefit of reaching a great number of people in a short time. However, it robs us of the benefits of face-to-face communications, the innumerable expressions and reactions in a person's voice and face. This can lead to carelessness with our written and spoken words. The Bible says, "Reckless words pierce like a sword" (Proverbs 12:18 NIV), and "a harsh word stirs up anger" (Proverbs 15:1 NIV).

Like William George Ravender, we can admire new technology and the ways in which it can help us, but we must not misuse it or let it control our lives. There is no better substitute for "the shining of a face upon a face" when witnessing to nonbelievers and when fellowshipping with one another.

✠

THEY DEVOTED THEMSELVES TO THE APOSTLES'
TEACHING AND TO THE FELLOWSHIP, TO THE
BREAKING OF BREAD AND TO PRAYER.

Acts 2:42 NIV

ABOUT WAITING

There are few things more worrying than sitting up for somebody, especially if that somebody be at a party. You cannot help thinking how quickly the time passes with them, which drags so heavily with you; and the more you think of this, the more your hopes of their speedy arrival decline. Clocks tick so loud, too, when you are sitting up alone, and you seem as if you had an under-garment of cobwebs on. First, something tickles your right knee, and then the same sensation irritates your left. You have no sooner changed your position, than it comes again in the arms; when you have fidgeted your limbs into all sorts of queer shapes, you have a sudden relapse in the nose, which you rub as if to rub it off—as there is no doubt you would, if you could. Eyes, too, are mere personal inconveniences; and the wick of one candle gets an inch and a half long, while you are snuffing the other. These, and various other little nervous annoyances, render sitting up for a length of time after everybody else has gone to bed, anything but a cheerful amusement.

This was just Mr. Dowler's opinion, as he sat before the fire, and felt honestly indignant with all the inhuman people at the party who were keeping him up. . . .

Mr. Dowler made up his mind that he would throw himself on the bed in the back room and think—not sleep, of course.

—The Pickwick Papers

Waiting can be difficult. Here, Mr. Dowler sits up at night, waiting for his wife to return from a party. He waits, impatiently imagining the good time she most certainly is having while he, miserable and deprived of sleep, suffers. Impatience adds to the trouble of waiting. Like Mr. Dowler's, our indignant thoughts toward those who keep us up can lead us to give up and give way to sleep.

So it was with the Israelites. They waited impatiently to enter the promised land. At the beginning of their journey, they believed God's promises to deliver them, and they trusted and praised Him. But when their journey became long, the Israelites became indignant. The Bible says, "[At first] they believed his promises and sang his praise. But they soon forgot what he had done and did not wait for his counsel. In the desert they gave in to their craving; in the wasteland they put God to the test" (Psalm 106:12–14 NIV).

Do you wait patiently for the Lord? It is hard to pray for something and then wait while those around us prosper. Psalm 37:7 tells us: "Be still before the LORD and wait patiently for him; do not fret when people succeed in their ways" (NIV). God's timing is always perfect. When we wait patiently for Him in hope, He will provide our every need.

✤

I WAIT FOR YOU, O LORD;
YOU WILL ANSWER, O LORD MY GOD.

Psalm 38:15 NIV

ANXIETY!

"My dear Alderman Cute," said Mr. Fish. ". . . The most dreadful circumstance has occurred. I have this moment received the intelligence. . . . The most frightful and deplorable event!"

"Fish!" returned the Alderman. "Fish! My good fellow, what is the matter? Nothing revolutionary, I hope! No—no attempted interference with the magistrates?"

"Deedles, the banker," gasped the Secretary. "Deedles Brothers—who was to have been here to-day—high in office in the Goldsmiths' Company—"

"Not stopped!" exclaimed the Alderman, "It can't be!"

"Shot himself . . . in his own counting house," said Mr. Fish, ". . . No motive. Princely circumstances!"

"Circumstances!" exclaimed the Alderman. "A man of noble fortune. One of the most respectable of men. Suicide, Mr. Fish! By his own hand!"

"This very morning," returned Mr. Fish.

"Oh the brain, the brain!" exclaimed the pious Alderman, lifting up his hands. "Oh the nerves, the nerves; the mysteries of this machine called Man! Oh the little that unhinges it: poor creatures that we are! Perhaps a dinner, Mr. Fish. Perhaps the conduct of his son, who, I have heard, ran very wild, and was in the habit of drawing bills upon him without the least authority! A most respectable man. One of the most respectable men I ever knew! A lamentable instance, Mr. Fish. A public calamity! I shall make a point of wearing the deepest mourning. A most respectable man! But there is One above. We must submit, Mr. Fish. We must submit!"

—The Chimes

The Chimes is one of a series of Christmas books Charles Dickens wrote, of which *A Christmas Carol* is the most well-known. Dickens wrote *The Chimes* in 1844 while he was living in Genoa, Italy. The melodramatic text reflects the anxiety-provoking social ills of the period—bad crops, miserable working conditions, child labor. "Oh the nerves, the nerves!"

Poor Deedles the banker might have lived if he had believed what Jesus taught in Luke 12:22–26: "Jesus said to his disciples: 'Therefore I tell you, do not worry about your life, what you will eat; or about your body, what you will wear. Life is more than food, and the body more than clothes. Consider the ravens: They do not sow or reap, they have no storeroom or barn; yet God feeds them. And how much more valuable you are than birds! Who of you by worrying can add a single hour to his life? Since you cannot do this very little thing, why do you worry about the rest?'" (NIV).

In these fast-moving times, it is impossible not to be anxious sometimes. The problem arises when we let anxiety control our lives. As Alderman Cute said, "But there is One above. We must submit." First Peter 5:6–7 instructs, "Humble yourselves therefore under God's mighty hand, that he may lift you up in due time. Cast all your anxiety on him because he cares for you" (NIV).

✤

THE LORD IS MY HELPER; I WILL NOT FEAR.
WHAT CAN MAN DO TO ME?

Hebrews 13:6

FIRE

The man looked at Nell again, and gently touched her garments, from which the rain was running off in little streams. "I can give you warmth," he said, after a pause; "nothing else. Such lodging as I have, is in that house," pointing to the doorway from which he had emerged, "but she is safer and better there than here. The fire is in a rough place, but you can pass the night beside it safely, if you'll trust yourselves to me. . . . See yonder there—that's my friend."

"The fire?" said the child.

"It has been alive as long as I have," the man made answer. "We talk and think together all night long."

The child glanced quickly at him in her surprise, but he had turned his eyes in their former direction, and was musing as before.

"It's like a book to me," he said . . . and many an old story it tells me. It's music, for I should know its voice among a thousand, and there are other voices in its roar. It has its pictures too. You don't know how many strange faces and different scenes I trace in the red-hot coals. It's my memory, that fire, and shows me all my life."

The child, bending down to listen to his words, could not help remarking with what brightened eyes he continued to speak and muse.

"Yes," he said, with a faint smile, "it was the same when I was quite a baby, and crawled about it, till I fell asleep."

—The Old Curiosity Shop

Nell Trent, a child of fourteen, and her elderly grandfather, left penniless after losing their old shop, wandered the streets begging for food and shelter. On a cold, rainy night, they met a stranger who took them in to his humble lodging to warm by the fire. There, the man shared stories about how the fire had become his friend.

The Bible holds stories that tell of God manifesting Himself in the form of fire. In Exodus 3, God appeared in the midst of a burning bush when He appointed Moses as the one to deliver the Israelites out of Egypt. God appeared as fire in Exodus 13:21, this time as a pillar of fire that led the Israelites in the night as they walked through the wilderness to the Red Sea. God also came down in the form of fire on Mount Sinai before He gave Moses the Ten Commandments (Exodus 19:18), and again He appeared as fire on an altar before Manoah (Samson's father) and his wife in Judges 13:17–22.

It is fitting that God so often chose to appear as fire, for they are similar in character: God's wrath can scorch and burn, if He so desires, but His love and mercy also provide us with comfort and warmth. Indeed, as the fire was to the stranger, God is our friend. Let the light of His Word shine in your life.

✿

HE SPREAD A CLOUD FOR A COVERING,
AND FIRE TO GIVE LIGHT IN THE NIGHT.

Psalm 105:39

EVERLASTING HOPE

I thought I had never seen the moon shine so white and ghastly anywhere, either on sea or on land, as she shone that night . . . When there was not much more than a boat's length between us, and the white light streamed cold and clear over all our faces, both crews rested on their oars with one great shudder, and stared over the gunwale of either boat, panic-stricken at the first sight of each other.

"Any lives lost among you?" I asked, in the midst of that frightful silence.

The men in the Long-bout huddled together like sheep at the sound of my voice.

"None yet . . . thanks be to God!" answered one among them.

And at the sound of his voice, all my men shrank together . . . without giving time for any more questions and answers, I commanded the men to lay the two boats close alongside of each other. When I rose up and committed the tiller to the hands of Rames, all my poor follows raised their white faces imploringly to mine. "Don't leave us, sir," they said, "don't leave us." "I leave you," says I, "under the command and the guidance of Mr. William Rames, as good a sailor as I am, and as trusty and kind a man as ever stepped. Do your duty by him . . . and remember to the last, that while there is life there is hope."

—The Wreck of the Golden Mary

W hile there is life there is hope." Perhaps you have heard this phrase before. The ancient Roman playwright Terence (ca. 195–159 BC) invented this proverb in a play called *Heauton Timoroumenos*. Dickens uses it here, in this scene from *The Wreck of the Golden Mary*, to encourage his characters during a very bleak moment in his tale.

We also have hope in our darkest times. The Bible tells us, "Surely there is a future, and your hope will not be cut off" (Proverbs 23:18 NASB). Jesus reminds us, "Everything is possible for him who believes" (Mark 9:23 NIV). There are many stories in the Gospels of people putting their hope in the Lord Jesus Christ. First Timothy 4:10 (NIV) says, "(For this we labor and strive), that we have put our hope in the living God, who is the Savior of all men, and especially of those who believe."

God is our everlasting hope. When we feel as if we are drowning in a sea of despair, we know that we can call on Him, and He hears us. His answer might not be what we expect, but, when we hope in God, we know that He will faithfully provide exactly what we need.

✠

THIS I RECALL TO MY MIND,
THEREFORE I HAVE HOPE:
THROUGH THE LORD'S MERCIES WE ARE NOT CONSUMED,
BECAUSE HIS COMPASSIONS FAIL NOT.
THEY ARE NEW EVERY MORNING;
GREAT IS YOUR FAITHFULNESS.

Lamentations 3:21–23

FACING ADVERSITY

I sat down in another room, before a girl, blind, deaf, and dumb; destitute of smell; and nearly so of taste: before a fair young creature with every human faculty, and hope, and power of goodness and affection, inclosed within her delicate frame, and but one outward sense—the sense of touch. There she was, before me; . . . with her poor white hand . . . beckoning to some good man for help, that an Immortal soul might be awakened. . . .

"When Laura is walking through a passage-way, with her hands spread before her, she knows instantly every one she meets, and passes them with a sign of recognition: but if it be a girl of her own age . . . There are questions and answers, exchanges of joy or sorrow, there are kissings and partings, just as between little children with all their senses. . . ."

Ye who have eyes and see not, and have ears and hear not; ye who are as the hypocrites of sad countenances, and disfigure your faces that ye may seem unto men to fast; learn healthy cheerfulness, and mild contentment, from the deaf, and dumb, and blind! Self-elected saints with gloomy brows, this sightless, earless, voiceless child may teach you lessons you will do well to follow. Let that poor hand of hers lie gently on your hearts; for there may be something in its healing touch akin to that of the Great Master whose precepts you misconstrue, whose lessons you pervert.

—American Notes for General Circulation

*C*harles Dickens met Laura Bridgman, a blind and deaf child, while he visited the Perkins Institution and Massachusetts School for the Blind in 1942. When he wrote *American Notes*, an account of his visit to North America, Dickens offered a powerful lesson on the subject of adversity—a lesson he took from the Bible.

In this passage, Dickens paraphrased a story found in Matthew 6:16–18, in which Jesus admonished those who took pleasure in publicly showing off their sacrifices. Jesus said, "When you fast, do not look somber as the hypocrites do, for they disfigure their faces to show men they are fasting. I tell you the truth, they have received their reward in full. But when you fast, put oil on your head and wash your face, so that it will not be obvious to men that you are fasting, but only to your Father, who is unseen; and your Father, who sees what is done in secret, will reward you" (NIV).

How we react to adversity can have a positive effect, not only on ourselves, but also on others. Facing adversity with faith and strength helps to lift us up. A positive attitude is contagious—an inspiration for others facing trials. It is pleasing to God when, to the best of our ability, we meet hard times with a cheerful heart.

✚

ALL THE DAYS OF THE AFFLICTED ARE EVIL,
BUT HE WHO IS OF A MERRY HEART HAS A CONTINUAL FEAST.

Proverbs 15:15

REGARDING STARS

There was once a child, and he . . . thought of a number of things. He had a sister, . . . his constant companion. These two used to wonder all day long. They wondered at the beauty of the flowers; they wondered at the height and blueness of the sky; they wondered at the depth of the bright water; they wondered at the goodness and the power of GOD who made the lovely world. . . .

There was one clear shining star that used to come out in the sky before the rest, near the church spire . . . It was larger and more beautiful . . . than all the others, and every night they watched for it, standing hand in hand at a window. Whoever saw it first cried out, "I see the star!" And often they cried out both together, knowing so well when it would rise, and where. . . . [B]efore lying down in their beds, they always looked out once again, to bid it good night; and when they were turning round to sleep, they used to say, "God bless the star!"

But while she was still very young . . . the sister . . . came to be so weak that she could no longer stand in the window at night; and then the child looked sadly out by himself, and when he saw the star, turned round and said to the patient pale face on the bed, "I see the star!" and then a smile would come upon the face, and a little weak voice used to say, "God bless my brother and the star!"

—*"A Child's Dream of a Star"*

Child's Dream of a Star" is one of Charles Dickens's early short stories. It is somewhat of a personal essay in that it was written in remembrance of Dickens's relationship with his sister, Fanny, who died a short time before he wrote it. As children, Dickens and Fanny spent time together gazing at the stars.

Stars are first mentioned in the Bible in Genesis. Genesis 1:16 tells us that God created the stars. When God made His covenant with Abram, He told Abram to look up at the stars. He said, "Count the stars if you are able to number them . . . So shall your descendants be" (15:5). The best-known star in the Bible is the star that appeared at Christ's birth: "Wise men from the East came to Jerusalem, saying, 'Where is He who has been born King of the Jews? For we have seen His star . . . and have come to worship Him'" (Matthew 2:1–2). "They departed; and behold, the star . . . went before them, till it came and stood over where the young Child was. When they saw the star, they rejoiced with exceedingly great joy" (vv. 9–10).

Today, we gaze at stars and wonder what lies beyond them. Like Dickens and his sister, we can only wonder. Scientists estimate there are more than ten billion trillion stars; yet, there is a God who calls each one by name (Psalm 147:4). That same God loves you and calls you by name.

✣

HE COUNTS THE NUMBER OF THE STARS;
HE CALLS THEM ALL BY NAME.

Psalm 147:4

HOSPITALITY

To-morrow was a bright and peaceful day; and nowhere were the autumn tints more beautifully seen, than from the quiet orchard of the Doctor's house. The snows of many winter nights had melted from that ground, the withered leaves of many summer times had rustled there . . . The honey-suckle porch was green again, the trees cast bountiful and changing shadows on the grass, the landscape was as tranquil and serene as it had ever been . . .

[Alfred Heathfield] had not become a great man; he had not grown rich; he had not forgotten the scenes and friends of his youth; he had not fulfilled any one of the Doctor's old predictions. But, in his useful, patient, unknown visiting of poor men's homes; and in his watching of sick beds; and in his daily knowledge of the gentleness and goodness flowering the by-paths of this world, not to be trodden down beneath the heavy foot of poverty, but springing up, elastic, in its track, and making its way beautiful; he had better learned and proved, in each succeeding year, the truth of his old faith. The manner of his life, though quiet and remote, had shown him how often men still entertained angels, unawares, as in the olden time; and how the most unlikely forms—even some that were mean and ugly to the view, and poorly clad—became irradiated by the couch of sorrow, want, and pain, and changed to ministering spirits with a glory round their heads.

—"The Battle of Life"

lfred Heathfield, ward of wealthy Dr. Jeddler, had not found greatness in his years as a doctor for the poor. Instead, he gleaned life lessons while he "entertained angels, unawares." As Dickens often did in his writing, he borrowed this phrase from the Bible. Hebrews 13:2: "Be not forgetful to entertain strangers: for thereby some have entertained angels unawares" (KJV).

"Entertain" in this verse means to be hospitable, to treat strangers in a warm, friendly, generous way. In Genesis 18, Abraham showed hospitality to three visitors. One he recognized as God, but the other two were unfamiliar. Abraham said, "Let a little water be brought, and then you may all wash your feet and rest under this tree. Let me get you something to eat, so you can be refreshed" (vv. 4–5 NIV). Later, we discover that these men with God were angels. They blessed Abraham with prophetic news: Abraham and his wife, Sarah, a childless couple, would soon have a son.

Showing hospitality to strangers often leads to unexpected blessings. As Alfred Heathfield discovered, entertaining "angels, unawares" can bring us life lessons and draw us closer to our faith. Even the "mean and ugly" have lessons to teach us about loving God and practicing hospitality. By extending Christian hospitality to others, we serve Jesus and glorify God the Father. And though you may expect nothing in return, you may find that your hospitality blesses you more than the one whom you serve.

✣

BE HOSPITABLE TO ONE ANOTHER WITHOUT GRUMBLING.

1 Peter 4:9

Managing Anger

The face that had humbled itself before [Harriet], looked on her now with such invincible hatred and defiance; and the hand that had gently touched her arm, was clenched with such a show of evil purpose, as if it would gladly strangle her . . .

"That I could speak with you, and not know you! . . ." said Alice, with a menacing gesture.

"What do you mean? What have I done?"

"Done!" returned [Alice]. "You have sat me by your fire; you have given me food and money; you have bestowed your compassion on me! You! Whose name I spit upon!"

The old woman, with a malevolence that made her ugliness quite awful, shook her withered hand at [Harriet] . . . , but plucked her by the skirts . . . , imploring her to keep the money.

"If I dropped a tear upon your hand, may it wither it up! If I spoke a gentle word in your hearing, may it deafen you! If I touched you with my lips, may the touch be poison to you! A curse upon this roof that gave me shelter! Sorrow and shame upon your head! Ruin upon all belonging to you!"

As she said the words, she threw the money down upon the ground, and spurned it with her foot. . . .

"I wouldn't take it if it paved my way to Heaven!" . . .

With a fierce action of her hand, as if she sprinkled hatred on the ground . . . she looked up once at the black sky, and strode out into the wild night.

—Dombey and Son

Money and a bad relationship are at the root of Alice's rage in this conversation with the benevolent Harriet Carker. When Alice was in need, Harriet had provided affection and as much money as she could afford. Alice was grateful until she realized that Harriet's brother is James Carker—a man with whom Alice shares a negative past. Then Alice explodes in a temper tantrum worthy of an Academy Award.

Angry emotions can be overwhelmingly powerful, and if we allow them to, they can control us. Proverbs 29:11 says, "A fool vents all his feelings, but a wise man holds them back." The Bible reminds us to get into the habit of thinking before we speak in anger: "Everyone should be quick to listen, slow to speak and slow to become angry, for man's anger does not bring about the righteous life that God desires" (James 1:19–20 NIV). Ephesians goes on to say, "Get rid of all bitterness, rage and anger, . . . Be kind and compassionate to one another, forgiving each other, just as in Christ God forgave you" (4:31–32 NIV).

When anger burns within us, there are several things that we can do. We can plan a constructive reconciliation, ask God to change our hearts, and most of all, model our behavior after Jesus Christ.

❦

Do not repay anyone evil for evil . . . If it is possible, as far as it depends on you, live at peace with everyone.

Romans 12:17–18 NIV

TEARS

I got up from the meal, saying . . . , "Well! I suppose I must be off!" and then I kissed my sister . . . , and kissed Biddy, and threw my arms around Joe's neck. . . .

I walked away at a good pace, thinking it was easier to go than I had supposed it would be . . . I whistled and made nothing of going. But the village was very peaceful and quiet, and the light mists were solemnly rising, as if to show me the world, and I had been so innocent and little there, and all beyond was so unknown and great, that in a moment with a strong heave and sob I broke into tears. It was by the finger-post at the end of the village, and I laid my hand upon it, and said, "Goodby, O my dear, dear friend!"

Heaven knows we need never be ashamed of our tears, for they are rain upon the blinding dust of earth, overlying our hard hearts. I was better after I had cried, than before—more sorry, more aware of my own ingratitude, more gentle. . . .

So subdued I was by those tears, and by their breaking out again in the course of the quiet walk, that when I was on the coach, and it was clear of the town, I deliberated with an aching heart whether I would not get down when we changed horses and walk back, and have another evening at home, and a better parting.

—Great Expectations

In *Great Expectations*, Dickens's character Pip reflects on a day in his adolescence when he left home for London. On that day, young Pip put aside his usual snobbish attitude, and he wept for the village and also the friends and family he left behind. Tears, he discovered, are nothing to be ashamed of.

Jesus also wept over a city. He cried on Palm Sunday as he approached Jerusalem, knowing what terrible events would happen there (Luke 19:41). He wept when His friend Lazarus died (John 11:35), and He must have wept when He learned that His cousin, John the Baptist, had been murdered (Mark 6). We can imagine that Jesus often shed tears. The prophet Isaiah says that He was "a Man of sorrows and acquainted with grief" (Isaiah 53:3). Certainly, then, Jesus understands when we cry.

God sees our tears, and He comforts us. The Bible tells us in Psalm 126:5, "Those who sow in tears shall reap in joy." God reminds us that our sadness will not last forever. One day He "will wipe every tear from [our] eyes. There shall be no more death, nor sorrow, nor crying" (Revelation 21:4). Do you hold back your tears, or do you let them flow? There is no sin or shame in crying. When we cry, we reflect a characteristic of our Lord Jesus Christ.

☦

NEVERTHELESS HE REGARDED THEIR AFFLICTION,
WHEN HE HEARD THEIR CRY.

Psalm 106:44

FINDING GOD

Jo, whose immediate object seems to be to get away on any terms, gives a shuffling nod. Mr. Guppy then throws him a penny, and Mrs. Snagsby calls to Guster to see him safely out of the house. But before he goes downstairs, Mr. Snagsby loads him with some broken meats from the table, which he carries away, hugging in his arms.

So, Mr. Chadband—of whom the persecutors say that it is no wonder he should go on for any length of time uttering such abominable nonsense, but that the wonder rather is that he should ever leave off, having once the audacity to begin—retires into private life until he invests a little capital of supper in the oil-trade. Jo moves on, through the long vacation, down to Blackfriars Bridge, where he finds a baking stony corner wherein to settle to his repast.

And there he sits, munching and gnawing, and looking up at the great cross on the summit of St. Paul's Cathedral, glittering above a red-and-violet-tinted cloud of smoke. From the boy's face one might suppose that sacred emblem to be, in his eyes, the crowning confusion of the great, confused city—so golden, so high up, so far out of his reach. There he sits, the sun going down, the river running fast, the crowd flowing by him in two streams—everything moving on to some purpose and to one end—until he is stirred up and told to "move on" too.

—*Bleak House*

In this scene from *Bleak House*, Mrs. Snagsby (the religious one) is being charitable; "fat and oily" Mr. Chadband (the preacher) is babbling about nothing; and Jo (the orphaned street sweeper) finds a spot near St. Paul's Cathedral to eat his meager lunch. Poor Jo—a boy void of religious education and relying on handouts to stay alive.

How does someone like Jo come to know God? Sometimes God leads us to Him by bringing people and circumstances into our lives. Other times, He instills a hunger in our hearts to know Him better. Jesus told this parable: "The kingdom of heaven is like a merchant looking for fine pearls. When he found one of great value, he went away and sold everything he had and bought it" (Matthew 13:45–46 NIV). That "pearl of great value" is believing by faith in the Lord Jesus Christ. Hebrews 11:6 says, "Anyone who comes to [God] must believe that he exists" (NIV).

Finding God is an exciting adventure that lasts a lifetime. It begins with believing He exists and then continues as we seek Him and yearn to know all that we can about Him. We learn about God through prayer and by meditating on scriptures from the Bible. We also learn through help from mature Christians. It is interesting to note that Jo dies in Dickens's novel—he dies as his doctor, Allan Woodcourt, leads him in reciting the Lord's Prayer. And just as with Jo, there truly is hope for us all.

❦

I LOVE THOSE WHO LOVE ME,
AND THOSE WHO SEEK ME DILIGENTLY WILL FIND ME.

Proverbs 8:17

PATIENCE IN HOPE

"I am afraid you have scarcely been a favourite with Papa," [Florence] said, timidly.

"There is no reason," replied Walter, smiling, "why I should be."

"No reason, Walter!"

"There was no reason," said Walter, understanding what she meant. "There are many people employed in the House. Between Mr. Dombey and a young man like me, there's a wide space of separation." . . .

"You may come back very soon," said Florence, "perhaps, Walter."

"I may come back," said Walter, "an old man, and find you an old lady. But I hope for better things."

"Papa," said Florence, after a moment, "will . . . speak more freely to me one day, perhaps; and if he should, I will tell him how much I wish to see you back again . . ."

There was a touching modulation in these words about her father, that Walter understood too well.

The coach being close at hand, he would have left her without speaking, for now he felt what parting was; but Florence held his hand . . .

"Walter," she said, looking full upon him with her affectionate eyes, "like you, I hope for better things. I will pray for them, and believe that they will arrive. . . . And now, God bless you, Walter! never forget me."

—Dombey and Son

Although Florence Dombey's father, Paul Dombey, pays little attention to his daughter, he does notice and does not approve when she becomes attracted to his employee Walter Gay. Mr. Dombey plots to separate the two by sending Walter to work in his firm in Barbados. Before parting, Walter and Florence exchange the hope that they will see each other again. Florence promises to pray about it, and as she puts her faith in God, she hopes to receive what she asks for.

Some situations may seem hopeless, but there is always hope in God. In the Bible we read about Job, sick and having lost everything but faith and hope in his heavenly Father. He cries out, "Oh, that I might have my request, that God would grant what I hope for" (Job 6:8 NIV). Job then waits for an answer. In time, the Lord lifts him from his life of despair and restores him to happiness and health. Psalm 31:24 reminds us to be courageous in hope for "He shall strengthen your heart, all you who hope in the LORD."

Hope requires patience. In Romans 8:24–25, we read: "But hope that is seen is no hope at all. . . . But if we hope for what we do not yet have, we wait for it patiently" (NIV). Indeed, God does not always give us what we hope for; instead He provides what we need. In Matthew 6:8, Jesus tells us, "For your Father knows the things you have need of before you ask Him." When our hope is in God, He will meet our needs in in His time, in His own way, and for His glory.

✠

LET YOUR MERCY, O LORD, BE UPON US,
JUST AS WE HOPE IN YOU.

Psalm 33:22

JOY!

Yes! and the bedpost was his own. The bed was his own, the room was his own. Best and happiest of all, the Time before him was his own, to make amends in!

"I will live in the Past, the Present, and the Future!" Scrooge repeated, as he scrambled out of bed. "The Spirits of all Three shall strive within me. Oh Jacob Marley! Heaven, and the Christmas Time be praised for this! I say it on my knees, old Jacob; on my knees! . . .

"I don't know what to do!" cried Scrooge, laughing and crying in the same breath; . . . "I am as light as a feather, I am as happy as an angel, I am as merry as a schoolboy. . . . A merry Christmas to everybody! A happy New Year to all the world. Hallo here! Whoop! Hallo!"

He had frisked into the sitting-room, and was now standing there: perfectly winded.

"There's the saucepan that the gruel was in!" cried Scrooge, start-ing off again, and going round the fireplace. "There's the door, by which the Ghost of Jacob Marley entered! There's the corner where the Ghost of Christmas Present, sat! There's the window where I saw the wandering Spirits! It's all right, it's all true, it all happened. Ha ha ha!"

Really, for a man who had been out of practice for so many years, it was a splendid laugh, a most illustrious laugh. The father of a long, long line of brilliant laughs!

—A Christmas Carol

A Christmas Carol has the most joyful ending of any of Charles Dickens's works. One can feel the happiness in this scene where Ebenezer Scrooge awakens with his life changed by the nighttime visits of three Christmas ghosts. For Scrooge, mirth and laughter are the result of a hard heart made merry. He drops to his knees, praising God and Christmastime—the season of Christ's birth—for turning his misery to joy.

Joy is found in Christ's presence. At the Feast of the Passover, after giving commandments to His disciples, Jesus said, "These things I have spoken to you, that My joy may remain in you, and that your joy may be full" (John 15:11). The Bible tells us "[God's] presence is fullness of joy" (Psalm 16:11). It instructs us to worship God joyfully: "Make a joyful shout to God, all the earth!" (Psalm 66:1). "Break forth in song, rejoice, and sing praises" (Psalm 98:4).

Our worship does not always have to be solemn or solitary. Sometimes, it is the right time to sing, shout, laugh, and praise God, as Ebenezer Scrooge did. Jesus said that when the Word of God is in our hearts, we receive it with joy (Luke 8:13). God our Father is the Creator of happiness. So, delight yourself in Him. As Christians, we should be the happiest people on Earth! Joy is good for us. Laugh, fill your heart with gladness, rejoice in the Lord, and be happy.

☩

A MERRY HEART DOES GOOD, LIKE MEDICINE.

Proverbs 17:22

SACRIFICE

Her friend parted his breakfast . . . with the child and her grandfather, and inquired whither they were going. She told him that they sought some distant country place remote from towns or even other villages, and with a faltering tongue inquired what road they would do best to take.

"I know little of the country," he said, shaking his head, . . . "But there are such places yonder."

"And far from here?" said Nell.

"Aye surely. . . ."

"We are here and must go on," said the child boldly; for she saw that the old man listened with anxious ears to this account.

"Rough people—paths never made for little feet like yours—a dismal blighted way—is there no turning back, my child!"

"There is none," cried Nell, pressing forward. "If you can direct us, do. If not, pray do not seek to turn us from our purpose. . . ."

"God forbid, if it is so!" said their uncouth protector, glancing from the eager child to her grandfather, who hung his head and bent his eyes upon the ground. "I'll direct you from the door, the best I can. . . ."

Before they had reached the corner . . . the man came running after them, and, pressing her hand, left something in it—two old, battered, smoke-encrusted penny pieces. Who knows but they shone as brightly in the eyes of angels, as golden gifts that have been chronicled on tombs?

—*The Old Curiosity Shop*

As Dickens's tale of *The Old Curiosity Shop* progresses, young Nell Trent and her grandfather are forced to leave their shop when an unpaid debt leaves them homeless. They wander the streets of London, dirty and cold and begging to survive. Friends help them from time to time. In this scene, the man's gift of two pennies must have seemed like a fortune to Nell and the old man.

The New Testament holds this story: As a way of honoring God, the Jews were instructed to give money to the temple and also to the poor. One day when Jesus and His disciples were at the temple, they observed a poor woman, a widow, enter and put two coins of little value into the offering box. The disciples were unimpressed. But Jesus said, "This poor widow has put in more than all the others. All these people gave their gifts out of their wealth; but she out of her poverty put in all she had to live on" (Luke 21:3–4 NIV).

The rich gave only part of what they had, but this woman gave all. No one noticed except God's Son. Jesus saw in her gift real sacrifice and selflessness. The widow may have been poor, but her simple gift showed a faith greater than gold. God doesn't look at the size of your gift; He looks at the size of your heart.

✣

HAS GOD NOT CHOSEN THE POOR OF THIS WORLD TO
BE RICH IN FAITH AND HEIRS OF THE KINGDOM WHICH
HE PROMISED TO THOSE WHO LOVE HIM?

James 2:5

OUR FATHER

His feeling about the child had been negative from her birth. He had never conceived an aversion to her: it had not been worth his while or in his humour. She had never been a positively disagreeable object to him. But now he was ill at ease about her. She troubled his peace. He would have preferred to put her idea aside altogether, if he had known how. Perhaps—who shall decide on such mysteries!—he was afraid that he might come to hate her.

When little Florence timidly presented herself, Mr. Dombey stopped in his pacing up and down and looked towards her. Had he looked with greater interest and with a father's eye, he might have read in her keen glance the impulses and fears that made her waver; the passionate desire to run clinging to him, crying, as she hid her face in his embrace, "Oh father, try to love me! there's no one else!" the dread of a repulse; the fear of being too bold, and of offending him; the pitiable need in which she stood of some assurance and encouragement; and how her overcharged young heart was wandering to find some natural resting-place, for its sorrow and affection.

But he saw nothing of this. He saw her pause irresolutely at the door and look towards him; and he saw no more. . . .

"Come here, Florence," said her father, coldly. "Do you know who I am?"

"Yes, Papa." . . . She looked down . . . and put out her trembling hand.

—Dombey and Son

r. Dombey wished to ignore his daughter, Florence. Their relationship was strained, at best. In this passage, Dickens crafts their conflicting emotions. Perhaps some of Dickens's own feelings are revealed here. He had a difficult relationship with his father. On the one hand, he held warm affection for him, but he hated that has father was a poor manager of money and ended up in a debtor's prison. At times, both Dickens and his character Florence must have felt fatherless.

Psalm 68:5 says that God is "a father of the fatherless." When, for whatever reason, our human parents fail us, we can trust God to care for us. King David wrote: "When my father and my mother forsake me, then the LORD will take care of me" (Psalm 27:10). Second Thessalonians 2:16 tells us that God the Father, through His grace, gives us "eternal encouragement and good hope" (NIV). And 1 John 3:1 reminds us that we are children of a loving God: "How great is the love the Father has lavished on us, that we should be called children of God! And that is what we are!" (NIV).

We need not be frightened or timid like poor little Florence, for we have a Father who is eager to spend time with us—through prayer and through His Word. Make time to spend with your Father today—He is waiting to hear from you.

✣

OUR FATHER IN HEAVEN,
HALLOWED BE YOUR NAME.

Matthew 6:9

BALANCE

Mr. Lorry's eyes were . . . attracted to [Carton's] face. Taking note of the wasted air which clouded the naturally handsome features, and having the expression of prisoners' faces fresh in his mind, he was strongly reminded of that expression.

"And your duties here have drawn to an end, sir?" said Carton, turning to him.

"Yes. . . . I have at length done all that I can do here." . . .

"Yours is a long life to look back upon, sir?" said Carton, wistfully.

"I am in my seventy-eighth year."

"You have been useful all your life; steadily and constantly occupied; trusted, respected, and looked up to?"

"I have been a man of business, ever since I have been a man. Indeed, I may say that I was a man of business when a boy."

"See what a place you fill at seventy-eight. How many people will miss you when you leave it empty!"

"A solitary old bachelor," answered Mr. Lorry, shaking his head. "There is nobody to weep for me." . . .

"If you could say, with truth, to your own solitary heart, to-night, 'I have secured to myself the love and attachment, the gratitude or respect, of no human creature; I have won myself a tender place in no regard; I have done nothing good or serviceable to be remembered by!' your seventy-eight years would be seventy-eight heavy curses; would they not?"

"You say truly, Mr. Carton; I think they would be."

—*A Tale of Two Cities*

Jarvis Lorry, an elderly banker who always practiced a strong work ethic, found himself alone and nearing the end of his life. Since boyhood, he had dedicated himself to business. He had done his work with morality, goodness, and honesty, but was it enough? Had Lorry's life been blessed by his commitment to his work, or cursed?

When we love anything more than we love God—work, spouse, children, relaxation, even our own lives—we are thrown out of balance. Psalm 127:1–2 says, "Unless the LORD builds the house, its builders labor in vain. Unless the LORD watches over the city, the watchmen stand guard in vain. In vain you rise early and stay up late, toiling for food to eat— for he grants sleep to those he loves" (NIV).

A good Christian life is a balanced life, with God at its center. When we choose to put God first, the rest of our life will fall into balance as we learn to set limits on that which takes up our time. To stay in balance, we should read the Gospels and study the way Jesus lived. His lifestyle is our example for living in perfect balance according to God's will.

⚜

THERE WAS A MAN ALL ALONE;
HE HAD NEITHER SON NOR BROTHER.
THERE WAS NO END TO HIS TOIL,
YET HIS EYES WERE NOT CONTENT WITH HIS WEALTH.
"FOR WHOM AM I TOILING," HE ASKED,
"AND WHY AM I DEPRIVING MYSELF OF ENJOYMENT?"

Ecclesiastes 4:8 NIV

WHAT IS LOVE?

"Charles Darnay! I rejoice to see you. We have been counting on your return . . ."

"I am obliged . . . ," he answered . . . to the Doctor. "Miss Manette—"

"Is well," said the Doctor, as he stopped short. . . . "She has gone out on some household matters, but will soon be home."

"Doctor Manette, I knew she was from home. I took the opportunity of her being from home, to beg to speak to you."

There was a blank silence.

"Yes?" said the Doctor, with evident constraint. ". . . speak on." . . .

"I hope the topic on which I am about to touch may not—"

He was stayed by the Doctor's putting out his hand to stop him. When he had kept it so a little while, he said, drawing it back:

"Is Lucie the topic?"

"She is."

"It is hard for me to speak of her at any time. It is very hard for me to hear her spoken of in that tone of yours, Charles Darnay."

"It is a tone of fervent admiration, true homage, and deep love, Doctor Manette!" he said deferentially. . . . "You anticipate what I would say, though you cannot know how earnestly I say it, how earnestly I feel it, without knowing my secret heart, and the hopes and fears and anxieties with which it has long been laden. Dear Doctor Manette, I love your daughter fondly, dearly, disinterestedly, devotedly. If ever there were love in the world, I love her."

—*A Tale of Two Cities*

ickens's works show that he had an idealistic view of love. Consider the string of adverbs he uses in this scene to describe how Charles Darnay loves Lucie Manette. Darnay loves Lucie *fondly*, *dearly*, *disinterestedly*, and *devotedly*. Think about the meanings of these words, and you might decide that they are hardly the most romantic ones that a person deeply in love would use to describe his tender feelings.

The Bible offers its own description of love. It says, "Love is patient, love is kind. It does not envy, it does not boast, it is not proud. It is not rude, it is not self-seeking, it is not easily angered, it keeps no record of wrongs. Love does not delight in evil but rejoices with the truth. It always protects, always trusts, always hopes, always perseveres" (1 Corinthians 13:4–7 NIV). These four scripture verses exist to tell us exactly what true love is.

These then are the adverbs that God uses to describe how Christians should love one another: patiently, kindly, unselfishly, humbly, honorably, gently, truthfully, protectively, trustingly, hopefully, and eternally. Yet, there is just one adverb that describes how God loves us—perfectly! It is God's perfect love that is the source of our own love, and we should endeavor to love others in the same way that He loves us.

✣

HE WHO DOES NOT LOVE DOES NOT KNOW GOD,
FOR GOD IS LOVE.

1 John 4:8

THE NEEDY

Mr. Squeers had before him a small measure of coffee, a plate of hot toast, and a cold round of beef; but he was at that moment intent on preparing breakfast for the little boys. . . .

"Conquer your passions, boys, and don't be eager after vittles." As he uttered this . . . , Mr. Squeers took a large bite out of the cold beef, and recognised Nicholas.

"Sit down, Mr. Nickleby," said Squeers. "Here we are, a breakfasting you see!"

Nicholas did NOT see that anybody was breakfasting, except Mr. Squeers . . .

"Ah!" said that gentleman, smacking his lips, . . . Think of the many beggars and orphans in the streets that would be glad of this [milk], little boys. A shocking thing hunger, isn't it, Mr. Nickleby?"

"Very shocking, sir," said Nicholas.

"When I say number one," pursued Mr. Squeers, putting the mug before the children, "the boy on the left . . . may take a drink; and when I say number two, the boy next him will go in, and so till we come to number five, which is the last boy. Are you ready?"

"Yes, sir," cried all the little boys with great eagerness.

"That's right," said Squeers, calmly getting on with his breakfast; "keep ready till I tell you to begin. Subdue your appetites, my dears, and you've conquered human nature. This is the way we inculcate strength of mind, Mr. Nickleby," said the schoolmaster, turning to Nicholas, and speaking with his mouth very full of beef and toast.

—The Life and Adventures of Nicholas Nickleby

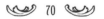

Wackford Squeers, the schoolmaster in Dickens's novel, took in needy, orphaned, and unwanted boys and then mistreated them. In this passage, he taunts the hungry boys with food while expounding the virtue of patience.

Jesus said this: "When the Son of Man comes in His glory, . . . all the nations will be gathered before Him, and He will separate them one from another . . . And He will set the sheep on His right hand, but the goats on the left. Then the King will say to those on His right hand, 'Come, you blessed of My Father, inherit the kingdom prepared for you . . . for I was hungry and you gave Me food; I was thirsty and you gave Me drink; I was a stranger and you took Me in; I was naked and you clothed Me; I was sick and you visited Me; I was in prison and you came to Me . . . Assuredly, I say to you, inasmuch as you did [these things] to one of the least of these My brethren, you did it to Me'" (Matthew 25:31–40).

When we help the needy, we honor God and glorify Jesus. Helping takes many forms—money, material items, compassionate favors, prayer. Let us ask God not only to bless those in need, but also to guide us in serving them.

✠

I KNOW THAT THE LORD WILL MAINTAIN
THE CAUSE OF THE AFFLICTED,
AND JUSTICE FOR THE POOR.

Psalm 140:12

CONCERNING SHYNESS

I can remember, when I was a very little girl indeed, I used to say to my doll when we were alone together, "Now, Dolly, I am not clever, you know very well, and you must be patient with me, like a dear!" And so she used to sit propped up in a great arm-chair, with her beautiful complexion and rosy lips, staring at me—or not so much at me, I think, as at nothing—while I busily stitched away and told her every one of my secrets.

My dear old doll! I was such a shy little thing that I seldom dared to open my lips, and never dared to open my heart, to anybody else. It almost makes me cry to think what a relief it used to be to me when I came home from school of a day to run upstairs to my room and say, "Oh, you dear faithful Dolly, I knew you would be expecting me!" and then to sit down on the floor, leaning on the elbow of her great chair, and tell her all I had noticed since we parted. I had always rather a noticing way—not a quick way, O no!—a silent way of noticing what passed before me and thinking I should like to understand it better. I have not by any means a quick understanding.

—Bleak House

Our narrator in this passage is Esther Summerson, the protagonist of Dickens's *Bleak House*. Esther grew up as a shy little girl being raised by her very strict aunt, Miss Barbary.

Merriam-Webster's Dictionary defines *shy* by using the following words and phrases: "easily frightened," "timid," "hesitant in committing oneself," "disposed to avoid a person or thing," "reserved," "secluded," "hidden." For those who struggle with shyness, speaking out boldly—even for the Lord—can be difficult. But the Bible reminds us that God did not create us to be timid and afraid (1 Timothy 1:7). As believers, we are to be the light of the world. Jesus asked, "Do people light a lamp and put it under a bowl? Instead they put it on its stand, and it gives light to everyone in the house. In the same way, let your light shine before men" (Matthew 5:14–16 NIV).

God has blessed each of His children with different gifts—some serving, teaching, or leading; others encouraging, giving, or showing mercy (Romans 12:6–8). Whatever gift we have been given, we should use it courageously, placing the emphasis on others rather than ourselves. When we encounter situations that prompt our fear and timidity, we can take heart from Deuteronomy 31:6: "Be strong and of good courage, do not fear nor be afraid of them; for the LORD your God, He is the One who goes with you. He will not leave you nor forsake you."

✣

PAUL . . . WELCOMED ALL WHO CAME TO SEE HIM. BOLDLY AND WITHOUT HINDRANCE HE PREACHED THE KINGDOM OF GOD AND TAUGHT ABOUT THE LORD JESUS CHRIST.

Acts 28:30–31 NIV

REGRET

"I very much regret," Martin resumed, looking steadily at him, and speaking in a slow and measured tone; "I very much regret that you and I held such a conversation together, as that which passed between us at our last meeting. I very much regret that I laid open to you what were then my thoughts of you, so freely as I did. The intentions that I bear towards you now are of another kind; deserted by all in whom I have ever trusted; hoodwinked and beset by all who should help and sustain me; I fly to you for refuge. I confide in you to be my ally; to attach yourself to me by ties of Interest and Expectation"—he laid great stress upon these words, though Mr. Pecksniff particularly begged him not to mention it; "and to help me to visit the consequences of the very worst species of meanness, dissimulation, and subtlety, on the right heads."

"My noble sir!" cried Mr. Pecksniff, catching at his outstretched hand. "And YOU regret the having harboured unjust thoughts of me! YOU with those grey hairs!"

"Regrets," said Martin, "are the natural property of grey hairs; and I enjoy, in common with all other men, at least my share of such inheritance. And so enough of that. I regret having been severed from you so long. If I had known you sooner, and sooner used you as you well deserve, I might have been a happier man."

—Life and Adventures of Martin Chuzzlewit

An old saying goes, "It is better to sleep on what you plan to do than to be kept awake by what you have done." We might assume from Martin Chuzzlewit's "grey hairs" that he had lost sleep while pondering his regrets.

The apostle Peter also struggled with regret. "Simon Peter asked [Jesus], 'Lord, where are you going?' Jesus replied, 'Where I am going, you cannot follow now, but you will follow later.' Peter asked, 'Lord, why can't I follow you now? I will lay down my life for you.' Then Jesus answered, 'Will you really lay down your life for me? Very truly I tell you, before the rooster crows, you will disown me three times!'" (John 13:36–38 NIV). Peter did just as Jesus had said, and afterward he "wept bitterly" (Luke 22:62 NIV). Peter regretted denying his friend.

Peter's regret led to something good—a stronger faith. He went on to become one of the leaders of the early church. Regrets do not have to follow us for the rest of our lives. Like Peter, when we feel regret deeply and choose to move forward in a better way, we can change regret to contentment.

⚜

ONE THING I DO, FORGETTING THOSE THINGS WHICH
ARE BEHIND AND REACHING FORWARD TO THOSE THINGS
WHICH ARE AHEAD, I PRESS TOWARD THE GOAL FOR THE
PRIZE OF THE UPWARD CALL OF GOD IN CHRIST JESUS.

Philippians 3:13–14

BAD COMPANY

"It was at that time that mama was most solicitous about my Cousin Maldon. I had liked him": [Annie] spoke softly, . . . "Very much. . . . If circumstances had not happened otherwise, I might have come to persuade myself that I really loved him, and might have married him, and been most wretched. There can be no disparity in marriage like unsuitability of mind and purpose."

I pondered on those words, even while I was studiously attending to what followed, as if they had some particular interest, or some strange application that I could not divine. "There can be no disparity in marriage like unsuitability of mind and purpose" . . .

"There is nothing," said Annie, "that we have in common. . . . If I were thankful to my husband for no more . . . I should be thankful to him for having saved me from the first mistaken impulse of my undisciplined heart."

She stood quite still . . . and spoke with an earnestness that thrilled me. Yet her voice was just as quiet as before. . . .

"When I was unhappy . . . I thought it would have become [Jack Maldon] better to have worked his own way on. I thought that if I had been he, I would have tried to do it . . . But I thought no worse of him, until the night of his departure for India. That night I knew he had a false and thankless heart. . . . I perceived, for the first time, the dark suspicion that shadowed my life."

—David Copperfield

There can be no disparity in marriage like unsuitability of mind and purpose." David Copperfield was confounded by these words—uncertain about what they meant. Mrs. Annie Strong, the much younger wife of Dr. Strong, headmaster of David's school, spoke them. Perhaps if David had consulted the Bible, he might have discovered their meaning.

The Bible cautions us to make wise choices about our relationships with others—not only whom we marry, but also those whom we choose as our friends. In 2 Corinthians 6:14 the apostle Paul wrote, "Do not be yoked together with unbelievers. For what do righteousness and wickedness have in common? Or what fellowship can light have with darkness?" (NIV). Paul also noted that "you must not associate with anyone who calls himself a brother but is sexually immoral or greedy, an idolater or slanderer, a drunkard or swindler. Do not even eat with such people" (1 Corinthians 5:11 NIV).

Paul encouraged us, as Christians, to be discerning, the way Annie Strong was. She observed Mr. Maldon's unchristian behavior and let him go. In this world, every day, we come in contact with both Christians and non-Christians. God does not forbid this, but rather He desires that we not get too close to unbelievers and risk being pulled into the enemy's snare.

⚜

DO NOT BE MISLED: "BAD COMPANY CORRUPTS
GOOD CHARACTER."

1 Corinthians 15:33 NIV

KIND WORDS

"Go you below, my love," said Mr. Murdstone. "David and I will come down, together. . . . David," he said, making his lips thin, by pressing them together, "if I have an obstinate horse or dog to deal with, what do you think I do?"

"I don't know."

"I beat him." . . .

I felt, in my silence, that my breath was shorter now. . . .

"What is that upon your face?"

"Dirt," I said.

He knew it was the mark of tears as well as I. But if he had asked the question twenty times, each time with twenty blows, I believe my baby heart would have burst before I would have told him so. . . .

God help me, I might have been improved for my whole life, I might have been made another creature perhaps, for life, by a kind word at that season. A word of encouragement and explanation, of pity for my child-ish ignorance, of welcome home, of reassurance to me that it was home, might have made me dutiful to him in my heart henceforth, instead of in my hypocritical outside, and might have made me respect instead of hate him. I thought my mother was sorry to see me standing in the room so scared and strange, and that, presently, when I stole to a chair, she followed me with her eyes more sorrowfully still—missing, perhaps, some freedom in my childish tread—but the word was not spoken, and the time for it was gone.

—David Copperfield

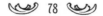

There are many painful scenes in the works of Charles Dickens. His words sometimes show readers what happens behind closed doors and in secret. This is one of those scenes. David Copperfield's stepfather, Mr. Murdstone, was a vicious man who enjoyed breaking the spirits of his wife and stepson. But, as Dickens so often does, he reveals through his characters a lesson about life. As David reflects on his childhood, he understands that kind words from his stepfather might have made David a different sort of man.

In Ephesians 4:15, the apostle Paul taught that speaking with love reflects the character of Christ: "We will speak the truth in love, growing in every way more and more like Christ" (NLT). Paul went on to say, in verse 29, "Do not let any unwholesome talk come out of your mouths, but only what is helpful for building others up according to their needs" (NIV). And in 1 Peter 3:10 we read: "Whoever would love life and see good days must keep his tongue from evil" (NIV).

Sometimes, out of weariness or frustration, we speak unkind words or let an opportunity pass when a gentle comment might have conveyed understanding and love. This happens to all of us; it comes with being human. Our words carry both power and potential. See if yours can lift someone up today.

✠

THE FEAR OF THE LORD IS TO HATE EVIL;
PRIDE AND ARROGANCE AND THE EVIL WAY
AND THE PERVERSE MOUTH I HATE.

Proverbs 8:13

JESUS

But hark! The Waits are playing . . . What images do I associate with . . . Christmas . . . as I see them set forth on the Christmas Tree? Known before all the others, keeping far apart from all the others . . . An angel, speaking to a group of shepherds in a field; some travellers, with eyes uplifted, following a star; a baby in a manger; a child in a spacious temple, talking with grave men; a solemn figure, with a mild and beautiful face, raising a dead girl by the hand; . . . calling back the son of a widow, on his bier, to life; a crowd of people looking through the opened roof of a chamber where he sits, and letting down a sick person on a bed, with ropes; the same, in a tempest, walking on the water to a ship; again, on a sea-shore, teaching a great multitude; again, with a child upon his knee, and other children round; . . . restoring sight to the blind, speech to the dumb, hearing to the deaf, health to the sick, strength to the lame, knowledge to the ignorant; . . . dying upon a Cross, watched by armed soldiers, a thick darkness coming on, the earth beginning to shake, and only one voice heard, "Forgive them, for they know not what they do." . . .

Let the benignant figure of my childhood stand unchanged! In every . . . image and suggestion that the season brings, may the bright star that rested above the poor roof, be the star of all the Christian World!

—*"A Christmas Tree"*

In his short story "A Christmas Tree," Charles Dickens reflected on what he called a "motley collection of odd objects, clustering on the [Christmas] tree." Among them are images of waits—traveling musicians—that turned Dickens's thoughts to Christmas songs and the life of Christ.

The Old Testament predicted Jesus' coming and events of His life: "But you, Bethlehem . . . , though you are little among the thousands of Judah, yet out of you shall come forth to Me the One to be Ruler in Israel, whose goings forth are from of old, from everlasting" (Micah 5:2). "Therefore the Lord Himself will give you a sign: Behold, the virgin shall conceive and bear a Son, and shall call His name Immanuel" (Isaiah 7:14). "Rejoice greatly . . . Behold, your King is coming to you . . . lowly and riding on a donkey" (Zechariah 9:9). "He was wounded for our transgressions, He was bruised for our iniquities; the chastisement for our peace was upon Him, and by His stripes we are healed" (Isaiah 53:5).

All of the things foretold about Jesus in the Old Testament did happen. The New Testament records those things and tells His story. Believing it—and in Him—is our only way to eternal life in heaven.

⚜

IF YOU CONFESS WITH YOUR MOUTH THE LORD JESUS
AND BELIEVE IN YOUR HEART THAT GOD HAS RAISED
HIM FROM THE DEAD, YOU WILL BE SAVED.

Romans 10:9

WORLDLINESS

The thoughts of worldly men are for ever regulated by a moral law of gravitation, which, like the physical one, holds them down to earth. The bright glory of day, and the silent wonders of a starlit night, appeal to their minds in vain. There are no signs in the sun, or in the moon, or in the stars, for their reading. They are like some wise men, who, learning to know each planet by its Latin name, have quite forgotten such small heavenly constellations as Charity, Forbearance, Universal Love, and Mercy, although they shine by night and day so brightly that the blind may see them; and who, looking upward at the spangled sky, see nothing there but the reflection of their own great wisdom and book-learning.

It is curious to imagine these people . . . , busy in thought, turning their eyes towards the countless spheres that shine above us, and making them reflect the only images their minds contain. The man who lives but in the breath of princes, has nothing his sight but stars for courtiers' breasts. The envious man beholds his neighbours' honours even in the sky; to the money-hoarder, and the mass of worldly folk, the whole great universe above glitters with sterling coin—fresh from the mint—stamped with the sovereign's head—coming always between them and heaven . . . So do the shadows of our own desires stand between us and our better angels, and thus their brightness is eclipsed.

—Barnaby Rudge

W orldliness" is defined in *Merriam-Webster's Dictionary* as: "of, relating to, or devoted to this world and its pursuits rather than to religion or spiritual affairs." In this passage from *Barnaby Rudge*, Charles Dickens offers a rich description of worldliness and how it separates us from God.

Jesus said, "No one can serve two masters. Either he will hate the one and love the other, or he will be devoted to the one and despise the other" (Matthew 6:24 NIV). The apostle Paul added: "If any of you thinks he is wise by the standards of this age, he should become a 'fool' so that he may become wise. For the wisdom of this world is foolishness in God's sight" (1 Corinthians 3:18–19 NIV).

The opposite of worldliness is heavenly mindedness. We cannot be both at the same time. When we are heavenly minded, we live with Christ as our model, believing that He died for our sins. Second Corinthians 5:17 describes it this way: "If anyone is in Christ, he is a new creation; old things have passed away; behold, all things have become new." When we set our minds on heavenly things, worldliness is no longer important to us. So choose to look up, keeping your eyes fixed on Christ and shifting your devotion from the world to God. Then watch as the glory of God unfolds in your life.

⚜

SET YOUR MIND ON THINGS ABOVE, NOT ON
THINGS ON THE EARTH.

Colossians 3:2

MOTHERS

God knows how infantine the memory may have been, that was awakened within me by the sound of my mother's voice in the parlour. . . . She was singing in a low tone. I think I must have lain in her arms, and heard her singing so to me when I was but a baby. The strain was new to me, and yet it was so old that it filled my heart brim-full; like a friend come back from a long absence.

I believed, from the solitary and thoughtful way in which my mother murmured her song, that she was alone. And I went softly into the room. She was sitting by the fire, suckling an infant, whose tiny hand she held against her neck. Her eyes were looking down upon its face, and she sat singing to it. I was so far right, that she had no other companion.

I spoke to her, and she started, and cried out. But seeing me, she called me her dear Davy, her own boy! and coming half across the room to meet me, kneeled down upon the ground and kissed me, and laid my head down on her bosom near the little creature that was nestling there, and put its hand to my lips.

I wish I had died. I wish I had died then, with that feeling in my heart! I should have been more fit for Heaven than I ever have been since.

—David Copperfield

When David Copperfield returned home, after being away at boarding school, the first sound he heard was that of his mother gently singing to his baby brother. In stark contrast to the cold indifference of David's school, Dickens created an image here of the comforting warmth of a mother's love. It so filled David's heart that he felt close to heaven.

This is how the Bible describes the role of women as wives and mothers. "A wife of noble character . . . is worth far more than rubies. Her husband has full confidence in her . . . She brings him good, not harm . . . She is clothed with strength and dignity; she can laugh at the days to come. She speaks with wisdom, and faithful instruction . . . She watches over the affairs of her household and does not eat the bread of idleness. Her children arise and call her blessed; her husband also, and he praises her: 'Many women do noble things, but you surpass them all.' . . . A woman who fears the LORD is to be praised. Give her the reward she has earned" (vv. 10–31 NIV).

God's love is mirrored in a mother's love. Both are available morning, noon, and night to address the family's needs. Through a mother's love, we can glimpse the nature of God's own love—nurturing, comforting, teaching, and disciplining us. So although the role of motherhood may seem mundane at times, it is a lofty calling created by the Lord and worthy of praise.

✤

YOUR MOTHER WAS LIKE A VINE IN YOUR
VINEYARD PLANTED BY THE WATER.

Ezekiel 19:10 NIV

REGARDING COMPASSION

The chill wind was howling, and the rain was falling, and the day was darkening moodily, when Harriet, raising her eyes from the work on which she had long since been engaged . . . saw . . . a solitary woman . . . miserably dressed; the soil of many country roads . . . clotted on her grey cloak by the streaming wet; no bonnet on her head, nothing to defend her rich black hair from the rain . . . She was fatigued, and after a moment . . . sat down upon a heap of stones; seeking no shelter from the rain, but letting it rain on her as it would. . . .

In a moment, Harriet was at the door . . . "You are very welcome to rest here. . . . Are you a stranger in this place?" asked Harriet.

"A stranger!" she returned, stopping between each short reply . . . "Yes. Ten or a dozen years a stranger. . . . Ten or a dozen years. I don't know this part. It's much altered since I went away."

"Have you been far?"

"Very far. Months upon months over the sea, and far away even then. I have been where convicts go," she added looking full upon her entertainer. "I have been one myself."

"Heaven help you and forgive you!" was the gentle answer.

"Ah! Heaven help me and forgive me!" she returned, nodding her head . . . "If man would help some of us a little more, God would forgive us all the sooner perhaps."

—Dombey and Son

It was not unusual for strangers to wander into Dickens's London and be lost in its lack of humanity. Harriet Carker, a gentle woman who lived quietly with her brother John, looked upon these strangers with kindness. When Alice Marwood wandered into Harriet's life on that cold, rainy day and admitted that she had been a convict, Harriet reacted compassionately.

The Bible tells a similar story. When the apostle Paul was imprisoned for preaching the gospel, only one man was kind to him, a Christian named Onesiphorus. Paul said, "[He] often refreshed me and was not ashamed of my chains" (2 Timothy 1:16 NIV). Compassion comes from knowing God and acting in ways that are pleasing to Him. Second Corinthians 1:3–4 says, "Praise be to the God and Father of our Lord Jesus Christ, the Father of compassion and the God of all comfort, who comforts us in all our troubles, so that we can comfort those in any trouble with the comfort we ourselves have received from God" (NIV).

When we come to God, He is kindhearted and forgiving. He requires us to be the same toward others. Harriet Carker noticed the strangers around her. When Alice Marwood was in need, Dickens tells us, "In a moment, Harriet was at the door." When strangers come into your life, are you like Harriet Carker? Do you meet them right away with earnest compassion?

☧

AND BE KIND TO ONE ANOTHER, TENDERHEARTED,
FORGIVING ONE ANOTHER, EVEN AS GOD IN
CHRIST FORGAVE YOU.

Ephesians 4:32

FORGIVENESS

"I have put the question to myself," said Edith . . . "and God knows I have met with my reply. Oh mother, mother, if you had but left me to my natural heart when I . . . was a girl . . . how different I might have been!"

Sensible that any show of anger was useless here, her mother restrained herself, and fell a whimpering, and bewailed that she had lived too long, and that her only child had cast her off, and that duty towards parents was forgotten in these evil days . . .

"Oh! The idea of your being my daughter, Edith, and addressing me in such a strain!"

"Between us, mother," returned Edith, mournfully, "the time for mutual reproaches is past."

"Then why do you revive it?" whimpered her mother. "You know that you are lacerating me in the cruellest manner. You know how sensitive I am to unkindness. At such a moment, too, when I have so much to think of, and am naturally anxious to appear to the best advantage! I wonder at you, Edith. To make your mother a fright upon your wedding-day! . . . such extremely cutting words—"

"They are past and at an end between us now," said Edith. "Take your own way, mother; share as you please in what you have gained; spend, enjoy, make much of it; and be as happy as you will . . . My lips are closed upon the past from this hour. I forgive you your part in to-morrow's wickedness. May God forgive my own!"

—Dombey and Son

dith Granger and her mother are arguing before Edith's wedding. Edith is angry that her mother raised her to lure rich gentlemen into marriage. Is Edith's forgiveness sincere at the end of this passage from *Dombey and Son*?

The Bible has much to say on the topic of forgiveness. It instructs us to forgive others as God forgave us through Jesus' death on the cross: "Bear with each other and forgive one another whatever grievances you may have against one another. Forgive as the Lord forgave you" (Colossians 3:13 NIV). It tells us that forgiveness is not always a onetime thing: "Peter came to Jesus and asked, 'Lord, how many times shall I forgive my brother when he sins against me? Up to seven times?' Jesus answered, 'I tell you, not seven times, but seventy-seven times' (Matthew 18:21–22 NIV). It also says that for us to be forgiven by God, we must first be forgiving: "For if you forgive other men when they sin against you, your heavenly Father will also forgive you. But if you do not forgive men their sins, your Father will not forgive your sins" (Matthew 6:14–16 NIV).

To offer forgiveness is an act of faith. And though we may not *feel* like forgiving, we can still *choose* to forgive. Consider these words from Corrie ten Boom, a holocaust survivor: "Forgiveness is an act of the will, and the will can function regardless of the temperature of the heart."

✠

FOR YOU, LORD, ARE GOOD, AND READY TO FORGIVE.

Psalm 86:5

THE GOOD KING

When King Lud saw the prince his son, and found he had grown up such a fine young man, he perceived what a grand thing it would be to have him married without delay, so that his children might be the means of perpetuating the glorious race of Lud, down to the very latest ages of the world. With this view, he sent a special embassy, composed of great noblemen who had nothing particular to do, and wanted lucrative employment, to a neighbouring king, and demanded his fair daughter in marriage for his son; stating at the same time that he was anxious to be on the most affectionate terms with his brother and friend, but that if they couldn't agree in arranging this marriage, he should be under the unpleasant necessity of invading his kingdom and putting his eyes out. To this, the other king (who was the weaker of the two) replied that he was very much obliged to his friend and brother for all his goodness and magnanimity, and that his daughter was quite ready to be married, whenever Prince Bladud liked to come and fetch her.

This answer no sooner reached Britain, than the whole nation was transported with joy. Nothing was heard, on all sides, but the sounds of feasting and revelry—except the chinking of money as it was paid in by the people to the collector of the royal treasures, to defray the expenses of the happy ceremony.

—The Pickwick Papers

harles Dickens wrote the last installments (published as monthly readings) of *The Pickwick Papers* in 1837, the same year Queen Victoria ascended to the British throne. In contrast to the king shown in this scene from Dickens's novel, Queen Victoria did not force selfish demands on her subjects. Instead, she had their best interests at heart, similar to the way God always acts in our best interests.

Far greater than any earthly king, God is the King of heaven; "[His] kingdom is not of this world" (John 18:36). Jesus told a parable about entering heaven: A great man planned a lavish banquet and invited many people. When the banquet day arrived, the invited guests decided not to come. The man said to his servants, "None of those . . . who were invited shall taste my supper" (Luke 14:24). So the man invited instead the poor and physically challenged, and anyone else who wanted to enter his kingdom and enjoy his feast.

Unlike the king in Dickens's story, God does not demand that we come to heaven, nor does He force His commands onto us. We have the choice of accepting His gift of eternal life or of walking away. God is a good King. His heaven is a place of exceeding joy (Jude 1:24) with no sadness (Revelation 21:4). He welcomes all into heaven who welcome His Son into their hearts.

✠

IF YOU CONFESS WITH YOUR MOUTH THE LORD JESUS
AND BELIEVE IN YOUR HEART THAT GOD HAS RAISED
HIM FROM THE DEAD, YOU WILL BE SAVED.

Romans 10:9

ABOUT GIVING

Always something in the nature of a Boil upon the face of society, Mr. Honeythunder expanded into an inflammatory Wen in Minor Canon Corner. Though it was not literally true . . . that he called aloud to his fellow-creatures: "Curse your souls and bodies, come here and be blessed!" still his philanthropy was of that gunpowderous sort that the difference between it and animosity was hard to determine. You were to abolish military force, but you were first to bring all commanding officers who had done their duty, to trial by court-martial for that offence . . . You were to abolish war, but were to make converts by making war upon them, and charging them with loving war as the apple of their eye. You were to have no capital punishment, but were first to sweep off the face of the earth all legislators, jurists, and judges, who were of the contrary opinion. You were to have universal concord, and were to get it by eliminating all the people who wouldn't, or conscientiously couldn't, be concordant. You were to love your brother as yourself, but after an indefinite interval of maligning him . . . Above all things, you were to do nothing in private, or on your own account. You were to go to the offices of the Haven of Philanthropy, and put your name down as a Member and a Professing Philanthropist. Then, you were to pay up your subscription, get your card of membership and your riband and medal, and were evermore to live upon a platform.

—The Mystery of Edwin Drood

Disingenuous philanthropists appear quite often in Dickens's novels. Mr. Luke Honeythunder is an example of one of these shady characters. Even his name is a dichotomy. Dickens portrays Mr. Honeythunder as loud, overbearing, self-important, and insincere.

If Jesus had been there to give unsolicited advice to Mr. Honeythunder, He might have repeated this from His Sermon on the Mount: "Be careful not to do your 'acts of righteousness' before men, to be seen by them. If you do, you will have no reward from your Father in heaven. . . . But when you give to the needy, do not let your left hand know what your right hand is doing, so that your giving may be in secret. Then your Father, who sees what is done in secret, will reward you" (Matthew 6:1–4 NIV). "In everything, do to others what you would have them do to you" (7:12).

Have you ever met a philanthropist? You have if you know God. He is the greatest philanthropist of all. James 1:17–18 tells us: "Every good and perfect gift is from above, coming down from the Father of the heavenly lights, who does not change like shifting shadows. He chose to give us birth through the word of truth, that we might be a kind of first fruits of all he created" (NIV). "The word of truth" is God's greatest gift to us—His son, Jesus Christ.

❧

GOD LOVES A CHEERFUL GIVER.

2 Corinthians 9:7

Concerning Integrity

I am doubtful whether I was at heart glad or sorry, when my school-days drew to an end . . .

My aunt and I had held many grave deliberations on the calling to which I should be devoted. For a year or more I had endeavoured to find a satisfactory answer to her often-repeated question, "What I would like to be?" But I had no particular liking, that I could discover, for anything. If I could have been inspired with a knowledge of the science of navigation, taken the command of a fast-sailing expedition, and gone round the world on a triumphant voyage of discovery, I think I might have considered myself completely suited. But, in the absence of any such miraculous provision, my desire was to apply myself to some pursuit that would not lie too heavily upon her purse; and to do my duty in it, whatever it might be. . . .

"I hope I shall be worthy of YOU, aunt. That will be enough for me." . . .

"But what I want you to be," . . . [said] my aunt, "—I don't mean physically, but morally; . . . is, a firm fellow. A fine firm fellow, with a will of your own. With resolution," said my aunt, shaking her cap at me . . ." With determination. With character, . . . with strength of character that is not to be influenced, except on good reason, by anybody, or by anything. That's what I want you to be. . . .

I hoped I should be what she described.

—David Copperfield

Miss Betsey Trotwood, David Copperfield's kindly aunt, had wise words for him as he set out into the world. More than David settling on a worthy calling, she wanted him to be a man with good morals and incorruptible integrity.

On integrity, the wise book of Proverbs tells us, "The righteous man walks in his integrity; his children are blessed after him" (20:7). Job, a man who lost everything and suffered much, is an example of a man who held on to integrity and did not give in to Satan's wiles. In Job 2:7–10 we read: "So Satan . . . struck Job with painful boils from the sole of his foot to the crown of his head. And he took for himself a potsherd with which to scrape himself while he sat in the midst of the ashes. Then his wife said to him, 'Do you still hold fast to your integrity? Curse God and die!' But he said to her, 'You speak as one of the foolish women speaks. Shall we indeed accept good from God, and shall we not accept adversity?'"

Even greater than Job's integrity was that of Jesus Christ. He always judged rightly; influenced people to live moral lives; and showed self-discipline, unwavering faith, and solid obedience to God. By reading the Bible and applying His example to our lives, we, too, can lead lives of integrity.

☙

THE INTEGRITY OF THE UPRIGHT WILL GUIDE THEM.

Proverbs 11:3

REAL LOVE

"Remember, Agnes? When I saw you, for the first time, coming out at the door, with your quaint little basket of keys hanging at your side?"

"It is just the same," said Agnes, smiling. "I am glad you think of it so pleasantly. We were very happy."

"We were, indeed," said I.

"I keep that room to myself still; but I cannot always desert Mrs. Heep, you know. And so," said Agnes, quietly, "I feel obliged to bear her company, when I might prefer to be alone. But I have no other reason to complain of her. If she tires me, sometimes, by her praises of her son, it is only natural in a mother. He is a very good son to her."

I looked at Agnes when she said these words, without detecting in her any consciousness of Uriah's design. Her mild but earnest eyes met mine with their own beautiful frankness, and there was no change in her gentle face.

"The chief evil of their presence in the house," said Agnes, "is that I cannot be as near papa as I could wish—Uriah Heep being so much between us—and cannot watch over him, if that is not too bold a thing to say, as closely as I would. But if any fraud or treachery is practising against him, I hope that simple love and truth will be strong in the end. I hope that real love and truth are stronger in the end than any evil or misfortune in the world."

—David Copperfield

Agnes Wickfield—a perfect daughter caring for her imperfect lawyer father. She never complains and is as sweet as the scent of a rose. Here, in her conversation with David Copperfield, Agnes wonders—though she doesn't come right out and say it—if her father's law clerk, Uriah Heep, has unworthy intentions. Still Agnes puts her hope in "real love and truth."

God's love is very real, and His truth is something that we can put our hope in. The apostle John wrote, "Grace, mercy, and peace will be with you from God the Father and from the Lord Jesus Christ, the Son of the Father, in truth and love" (2 John 1:3). God's love for us is love that we can believe in. John also wrote: "And we have known and believed the love that God has for us. God is love, and he who abides in love abides in God, and God in him" (1 John 4:16).

Like Agnes, we should put our hope in real love and truth. Romans 5:5 says, "Hope does not disappoint us, because God has poured out his love into our hearts by the Holy Spirit, whom he has given us" (NIV). Do you believe that God's love is truly real? In the words of the apostle Paul: "I pray that you, being rooted and established in love, may have power . . . to grasp how wide and long and high and deep is the love of Christ" (Ephesians 3:17–18 NIV).

✣

HOW PRICELESS IS YOUR UNFAILING LOVE!

Psalm 36:7 NIV

PROCRASTINATION

I passed my evenings with Mr. and Mrs. Micawber, during the remaining term of our residence under the same roof; and I think we became fonder of one another as the time went on. On the last Sunday, they invited me to dinner . . . We had a very pleasant day, though we were all in a tender state about our approaching separation.

"I shall never, Master Copperfield," said Mrs. Micawber, "revert to the period when Mr. Micawber was in difficulties, without thinking of you. Your conduct has always been of the most delicate and obliging description. You have never been a lodger. You have been a friend." . . .

I . . . said I was very sorry we were going to lose one another.

"My dear young friend," said Mr. Micawber, "I am older than you; a man of some experience in life, and—and of some experience . . . in difficulties . . . I have nothing to bestow but advice. Still my advice is so far worth taking, that—in short, that I have never taken it myself, and am the"—here Mr. Micawber, who had been beaming and smiling, all over his head and face, up to the present moment, checked himself and frowned—"the miserable wretch you behold."

"My dear Micawber!" urged his wife.

"I say," returned Mr. Micawber, quite forgetting himself, and smiling again, "the miserable wretch you behold. My advice is, never do tomorrow what you can do today. Procrastination is the thief of time. Collar him!"

—David Copperfield

"Never put off till tomorrow what you can do today." Thomas Jefferson said it, Lincoln paraphrased it, and Dickens repeated it through his character Mr. Micawber. He passed this counsel on to young David Copperfield, knowing firsthand that his advice was good.

Jesus also offered wise advice on the subject of procrastination. In Luke 9:61, a man said to Jesus, "I will follow you, Lord; but first let me go back and say goodbye to my family" (NIV). Jesus replied, "No one who puts his hand to the plow and looks back is fit for service in the kingdom of God" (v. 62 NIV). And James 4:13–14 connects to Dickens's phrase "Procrastination is the thief of time" when it says: "You who say, 'Today or tomorrow we will go to this or that city . . .' Why, you do not even know what will happen tomorrow. . . . You are a mist that appears for a little while and then vanishes" (NIV).

We all procrastinate sometimes, but we should not procrastinate when it comes to learning more about God and doing His work. God uses His Christian sons and daughters to carry out His will. When we put off reading our Bibles, going to church, and helping others, we also put off God. Think of Mr. Micawber's advice and consider what you can do to make wise use of your time this day.

✣

HE WHO OBSERVES THE WIND WILL NOT SOW,
AND HE WHO REGARDS THE CLOUDS WILL NOT REAP.

Ecclesiastes 11:4

HARD-HEARTEDNESS

Oh! But he was a tight-fisted hand at the grindstone, Scrooge! a squeezing, wrenching, grasping, scraping, clutching, covetous, old sinner! Hard and sharp as flint, from which no steel had ever struck out generous fire; secret, and self-contained, and solitary as an oyster. The cold within him froze his old features, nipped his pointed nose, shrivelled his cheek, stiffened his gait; made his eyes red, his thin lips blue; and spoke out shrewdly in his grating voice. A frosty rime was on his head, and on his eyebrows, and his wiry chin. He carried his own low temperature always about with him; he iced his office in the dog-days; and didn't thaw it one degree at Christmas.

External heat and cold had little influence on Scrooge. No warmth could warm, no wintry weather chill him. No wind that blew was bitterer than he, no falling snow was more intent upon its purpose, no pelting rain less open to entreaty. Foul weather didn't know where to have him. . . .

Nobody ever stopped him in the street to say, with gladsome looks, "My dear Scrooge, how are you? When will you come to see me?" No beggars implored him to bestow a trifle, no children asked him what it was o'clock, no man or woman ever once in all his life inquired the way to such and such a place, of Scrooge. . . .

But what did Scrooge care! It was the very thing he liked.

—A Christmas Carol

ickens's Scrooge became such a popular character that *Merriam-Webster's Dictionary* lists his surname as a noun meaning "miserly person." Tightfisted and hard-hearted—that was Ebenezer Scrooge. Dickens created his protagonist in *A Christmas Carol* to despise the poor, and certainly that gave the author motivation to tell the tale of a callous heart transformed.

In Exodus 7–8, we find a prime example of a hard heart. Pharaoh, the evil dictator who enslaved the Israelites and refused to let them go, ignored God's warnings. He rebelled against God many times with a hardened heart, and finally the Lord punished him severely. In Mark 8:17–18, Jesus compares a hardened heart to being spiritually blind. "Why are you talking about having no bread? Do you still not see or understand? Are your hearts hardened? Do you have eyes but fail to see, and ears but fail to hear?" (NIV). Jesus was chastising his disciples for not remembering the miracle He performed when feeding the four thousand (Mark 8:1–9).

Our hearts become hard when we go about our own way instead of following what God wants us to do. But a hard heart need not be forever. God is eager to soften our hearts and forgive our sins. In Ezekiel 36:26, He says, "I will give you a new heart and put a new spirit in you; I will remove from you your heart of stone and give you a heart of flesh" (NIV).

✣

AS WATER REFLECTS A FACE,
SO A MAN'S HEART REFLECTS THE MAN.

Proverbs 27:19 NIV

ABOUT FRIENDSHIP

Martin began to work at the grammar-school next morning, with so much vigour and expedition, that Mr. Pinch had new reason to do homage to the natural endowments of that young gentleman, and to acknowledge his infinite superiority to himself. The new pupil received Tom's compliments very graciously; and having by this time conceived a real regard for him, in his own peculiar way, predicted that they would always be the very best of friends, and that neither of them, he was certain (but particularly Tom), would ever have reason to regret the day on which they became acquainted. Mr. Pinch was delighted to hear him say this, and felt so much flattered by his kind assurances of friendship and protection, that he was at a loss how to express the pleasure they afforded him. And indeed it may be observed of this friendship, such as it was, that it had within it more likely materials of endurance than many a sworn brotherhood that has been rich in promise; for so long as the one party found a pleasure in patronizing, and the other in being patronised (which was in the very essence of their respective characters), it was of all possible events among the least probable, that the twin demons, Envy and Pride, would ever arise between them. So in very many cases of friendship, or what passes for it, the old axiom is reversed, and like clings to unlike more than to like.

—Life and Adventures of Martin Chuzzlewit

Dickens's works are filled with interesting and unlikely friendships. When Dickens wrote about the friendship between Martin Chuzzlewit and Tom Pinch, he might have drawn elements from his own friendships. Dickens's circle of friends included Hans Christian Andersen, Henry Wadsworth Longfellow, and his best friend, the English novelist Wilkie Collins.

The Bible also contains many interesting stories about friendship. The most well-known is that of David and Jonathan in 1 Samuel 20. Their relationship held no jealousy. They were loyal friends, supportive and protective of each other. They were so committed to each other that they pledged to be friends for life. Even after Jonathan was killed, David honored their friendship by looking after Jonathan's family.

Solid friendships are a gift from God. But His greatest gift is our friendship with Jesus Christ—the One who loved us so much that He gave His life for our salvation. This is what Jesus said to His disciples: "You are my friends if you do what I command. I no longer call you servants, because a servant does not know his master's business. Instead, I have called you friends, for everything that I learned from my Father I have made known to you. You did not choose me, but I chose you" (John 15:14–16 NIV). When we choose to believe in Him, Jesus chooses to be our friend—the very best Friend.

✤

"GREATER LOVE HAS NO ONE THAN THIS, THAN TO LAY DOWN ONE'S LIFE FOR HIS FRIENDS."

John 15:13

ENVY

How well she looked? Well? Why, if he had exhausted every laudatory adjective in the dictionary, it wouldn't have been praise enough. When and where was there ever such a plump, roguish, comely, bright-eyed, enticing, bewitching, captivating, maddening little [woman] in all this world, as Dolly! What was the Dolly of five years ago, to the Dolly of that day! How many coachmakers, saddlers, cabinet-makers, and professors of other useful arts, had deserted their fathers, mothers, sisters, brothers, and . . . their cousins, for the love of her! How many unknown gentlemen—supposed to be of mighty fortunes, if not titles—had waited round the corner after dark . . . to deliver offers of marriage folded up in love-letters! . . . How had she recruited the king's service, both by sea and land, through rendering desperate his loving subjects between the ages of eighteen and twenty-five! How many young ladies had publicly professed, with tears in their eyes, that for their tastes she was much too short, too tall, too bold, too cold, too stout, too thin, too fair, too dark—too everything but handsome! How many old ladies, taking counsel together, had thanked Heaven their daughters were not like her, and had hoped she might come to no harm, and had thought she would come to no good, and had wondered what people saw in her, and had arrived at the conclusion that she was "going off" in her looks . . . and that she was a thorough imposition and a popular mistake!

—Barnaby Rudge

William Shakespeare wrote, in his play *Othello*, "And oft, my jealousy shapes faults that are not." So did the young ladies of Chigwell shape the faults of Dolly Varden. Dickens's use of adjectives in this passage from *Barnaby Rudge* contrasts Dolly's positive attributes with the negative ones formed by the envious ladies.

James spoke about envy as he cautioned, "If you harbor bitter envy and selfish ambition in your hearts, do not boast about it or deny the truth. Such 'wisdom' does not come down from heaven but is earthly, unspiritual, of the devil. For where you have envy and selfish ambition, there you find disorder and every evil practice" (3:14–16 NIV). The Bible holds many examples of evil acts that have resulted from envy. Read about the jealousy between the brothers Jacob and Esau (Genesis 25–27), Joseph and his tunic of many colors (Genesis 37), and King Saul's jealous anger toward David (1 Samuel 15–21). The book of Proverbs even suggests that envy might adversely affect one's health (14:30).

Envy is not a product of love, for love "does not envy, it does not boast, it is not proud" (1 Corinthians 13:4 NIV). To avoid self-seeking envy, we must follow our Lord's example found in 1 Samuel 16:7: "The LORD does not look at the things man looks at. Man looks at the outward appearance, but the LORD looks at the heart" (NIV).

❧

LET US NOT BECOME CONCEITED, PROVOKING ONE
ANOTHER, ENVYING ONE ANOTHER.

Galatians 5:26

OLD AGE

The traveller . . . holding the light near to his panting and reeking beast, examined [the horse] in limb and carcass. Meanwhile, the other man sat very composedly in his vehicle, which was a kind of chaise with a depository for a large bag of tools, and watched his proceedings with a careful eye.

The looker-on was a round, red-faced, sturdy yeoman, with a double chin, and a voice husky with good living, good sleeping, good humour, and good health. He was past the prime of life, but Father Time is not always a hard parent, and, though he tarries for none of his children, often lays his hand lightly upon those who have used him well; making them old men and women inexorably enough, but leaving their hearts and spirits young and in full vigour. With such people the grey head is but the impression of the old fellow's hand in giving them his blessing, and every wrinkle but a notch in the quiet calendar of a well-spent life.

The person whom the traveller had so abruptly encountered was of this kind: bluff, hale, hearty, and in a green old age: at peace with himself, and evidently disposed to be so with all the world. Although muffled up in divers coats and handkerchiefs . . . there was no disguising his plump and comfortable figure; neither did certain dirty finger-marks upon his face give it any other than an odd and comical expression, through which its natural good humour shone with undiminished lustre.

—Barnaby Rudge

Dickens knew the worth of maturity. Many of his elderly characters are fully engaged in life, like the yeoman in *Barnaby Rudge* so eloquently described by the author. There are more than 120 elderly characters in Dickens's works, and he avoids portraying them as stereotypical.

God also values the elderly. In Leviticus 19:32, He makes this command: "Rise in the presence of the aged, show respect for the elderly and revere your God. I am the LORD" (NIV). God often used senior citizens to accomplish His work: Elizabeth was very old when she gave birth to John the Baptist (Luke 1:7), Moses and his brother, Aaron, were in their eighties when God sent them to ask Pharaoh to release the Israelites (Exodus 7:7), and Joshua remained active in God's army until he died at the age of 110 (Joshua 24:29)!

When Dickens described his yeoman as being in "a green old age," his inspiration may have come from Psalm 92:14: "They still bear fruit in old age; they are ever full of sap and green" (ESV). Length of years does not release us from our responsibilities as Christians. As long as we live, we are still to bear fruit for God. The elderly people in our lives can be a source of wisdom and inspiration. And so should we strive to be as we grow to "a green old age."

⚜

AGE SHOULD SPEAK,
AND MULTITUDE OF YEARS SHOULD TEACH WISDOM.

Job 32:7

REGARDING CONTENTMENT

"YOU know you must keep up your spirits, mother, and not be lonesome because I'm not at home. I shall very often be able to look in when I come into town . . . , and I shall send you a letter sometimes, and when the quarter comes round, I can get a holiday of course; and then see if we don't take little Jacob to the play. . . ."

"I hope plays mayn't be sinful, Kit, but I'm a'most afraid," said Mrs. Nubbles.

"I know who has been putting that in your head," rejoined her son disconsolately; "that's Little Bethel again. Now I say, mother, pray don't take to going there regularly, for if I was to see your good-humoured face that has always made home cheerful, turned into a grievous one, and the baby trained to look grievous too, . . . if I was to see this, and see little Jacob looking grievous likewise, I should so take it to heart that I'm sure I should go and list for a soldier, and run my head on purpose against the first cannon-ball I saw coming my way."

"Oh, Kit, don't talk like that."

"I would, indeed, mother, and unless you want to make me feel very wretched and uncomfortable, you'll keep that bow on your bonnet, which you'd more than half a mind to pull off last week. Can you sup-pose there's any harm in looking as cheerful and being as cheerful as our poor circumstances will permit?

—The Old Curiosity Shop

Kit Nubbles, shop boy at the Old Curiosity Shop, was concerned about his widowed mother's attitude. She always worried over whether or not what she and her children did was right and pleasing to God. But she worried overly so, and Kit was afraid that his mother, unknowingly, taught her children to be unhappy.

Of course, we should try our best to live a solid Christian life, but in doing so, we should also be content with our trying and not worry excessively that it is not enough. Contentment is a gift from God. It comes when our hearts find peace knowing that God is in control and that He loves us in spite of our imperfections. Romans 3:23 reminds us that "all have sinned and fall short of the glory of God." As hard as we try, we cannot perfectly please Him. Fortunately, our contentment depends not on being perfect, but rather on accepting that we are not.

In the New Testament, we read that Jesus came into the world so that we might have life and "have it more abundantly" (John 10:10). He came not to condemn, but to free. When we do our Christian best and accept God's mercy and forgiveness, then our hearts are free to be content, and we can put on a cheerful face in all of our circumstances.

✣

I HAVE LEARNED IN WHATEVER STATE I AM, TO BE CONTENT.

Philippians 4:11

ON PARENTING

After tea there was a walk in the garden, and the evening being very fine they strolled out at the garden-gate into some lanes and bye-roads, and sauntered up and down until it grew quite dark. The time seemed to pass very quickly with all the party. Kate went first, leaning upon her brother's arm, and talking with him and Mr. Frank Cheeryble; and Mrs. Nickleby and the elder gentleman followed at a short distance, the kindness of the good merchant, his interest in the welfare of Nicholas, and his admiration of Kate, so operating upon the good lady's feelings, that the usual current of her speech was confined within very narrow and circumscribed limits. Smike . . . accompanied them, joining sometimes one group and some-times the other, as brother Charles, laying his hand upon his shoulder, bade him walk with him, or Nicholas, looking smilingly round, beckoned him to come and talk with the old friend who understood him best, and who could win a smile into his careworn face when none else could.

Pride is one of the seven deadly sins; but it cannot be the pride of a mother in her children, for that is a compound of two cardinal vir-tues—faith and hope. This was the pride which swelled Mrs. Nickleby's heart that night, and this it was which left upon her face, glistening in the light when they returned home, traces of the most grateful tears she had ever shed.

—The Life and Adventures of Nicholas Nickleby

harles H. Spurgeon once said, "You may speak but a word to a child, and in that child there may be slumbering a noble heart which shall stir the Christian Church in years to come." Seeing your child grow into an adult with a noble heart would fill any parent with pride, just as Mrs. Nickleby was very proud of her children.

The Bible offers wise advice for parents. When he gave the Ten Commandments to the Israelites, Moses said, "These commandments that I give you today are to be on your hearts. Impress them on your children. Talk about them when you sit at home and when you walk along the road, when you lie down and when you get up. Tie them as symbols on your hands and bind them on your foreheads. Write them on the doorframes of your houses and on your gates" (Deuteronomy 6:6–9 NIV). Proverbs 22:6 adds: "Train a child in the way he should go, and when he is old he will not turn from it" (NIV).

Dickens wrote that having pride in your children is not a sin, but rather the result of ongoing faith and hope. For it is faith and hope in the Lord that should form the foundation for raising children in a godly home.

❧

DO NOT EXASPERATE YOUR CHILDREN;
INSTEAD, BRING THEM UP IN THE TRAINING
AND INSTRUCTION OF THE LORD.

Ephesians 6:4 NIV

DIFFICULT PEOPLE

Mrs. Varden was a lady of what is commonly called an uncertain temper—a phrase which being interpreted signifies a temper tolerably certain to make everybody more or less uncomfortable. Thus it generally happened, that when other people were merry, Mrs. Varden was dull; and that when other people were dull, Mrs. Varden was disposed to be amazingly cheerful. Indeed the worthy housewife was of such a capricious nature, that she not only attained a higher pitch of genius than Macbeth, in respect of her ability to be wise, amazed, temperate and furious, loyal and neutral in an instant, but would sometimes ring the changes backwards and forwards on all possible moods and flights in one short quarter of an hour; performing, as it were, a kind of triple bob major on the peal of instruments in the female belfry, with a skilfulness and rapidity of execution that astonished all who heard her.

It had been observed in this good lady (who did not want for personal attractions, being plump and buxom to look at, though like her fair daughter, somewhat short in stature) that this uncertainty of disposition strengthened and increased with her temporal prosperity; . . . Whether they were right or wrong in this conjecture, certain it is that minds, like bodies, will often fall into a pimpled ill-conditioned state from mere excess of comfort, and like them, are often successfully cured by remedies in themselves very nauseous and unpalatable.

—Barnaby Rudge

Martha Varden, the locksmith's wife in *Barnaby Rudge*, was undeniably a woman of many moods and difficult to be around. Perhaps you know or work with someone just like her, someone with a temper and moods that shift like the wind.

Jesus often dealt with difficult people. He was criticized, made fun of, and pursued by an angry mob. Still, His message to us is: "Love your enemies, do good to those who hate you, bless those who curse you, pray for those who mistreat you" (Luke 6:27–28 NIV). God's way of dealing with difficult people is often difficult! Philippians 2:3 says that we should react with humility and think of others as better than ourselves, and Proverbs 12:16 tells us that "a fool shows his annoyance at once, but a prudent man overlooks an insult" (NIV). God wants us to use the tools of humility, patience, and love when difficult people cross our paths.

Dealing with a problematic family member, store clerk, or coworker certainly tests our faith, but living or working with individuals like Mrs. Varden can be made easier when we ask God to change our hearts, to allow us to see them as needing love, mercy, and understanding. When we imitate Christ's patience and humility, we learn to see even difficult people as God sees them—children of the King.

✣

CLOTHE YOURSELVES WITH TENDERHEARTED MERCY,
KINDNESS, HUMILITY, GENTLENESS, AND PATIENCE.
MAKE ALLOWANCE FOR EACH OTHER'S FAULTS, AND
FORGIVE ANYONE WHO OFFENDS YOU.

Colossians 3:12–13 NLT

FAMILY QUARRELS

"It's a devil of a thing . . ." said Mr. Swiveller, "when relations fall out and disagree. If the wing of friendship should never moult a feather, the wing of relationship should never be clipped, but be always expanded and serene. Why should a grandson and grandfather peg away at each other with mutual wiolence when all might be bliss and concord. Why not jine hands and forget it?" . . .

The jolly old grandfather says to the wild young grandson, "I have brought you up and educated you . . . ; I have put you in the way of getting on in life; you have bolted a little out of course, as young fellows often do; and you shall never have another chance, nor the ghost of half a one." The wild young grandson makes answer to this and says, "You're as rich as rich can be; you have been at no uncommon expense on my account, you're saving up piles of money for my little sister . . . why can't you stand a trifle for your grown-up relation?" The jolly old grandfather . . . retorts, not only that he declines to fork out with that cheerful readiness which is always so agreeable and pleasant in a gentleman of his time of life, but that he will bow up, and call names, and make reflections whenever they meet. Then the plain question is, an't it a pity that this state of things should continue?

—The Old Curiosity Shop

Family quarrels often occur over jealousy, as in this scene from Dickens's *The Old Curiosity Shop*. In fact, similar situations occur in stories from the Bible.

Take Jacob and Esau, for instance (Genesis 25). These twin brothers fought over their inheritance and hated each other for many years. Then, in Genesis 37, we read that Joseph's brothers hated him because their father favored Joseph. They hated Joseph so much that they planned to kill him. The Bible asks in Romans 14:10, "Why do you judge your brother? Or why do you look down on your brother? For we will all stand before God's judgment seat" (NIV). Jesus' disciple John tells us in 1 John 4:20 that family quarrels separate us from God: "If anyone says, 'I love God,' yet hates his brother, he is a liar. For anyone who does not love his brother, whom he has seen, cannot love God, whom he has not seen" (NIV).

Mr. Swiveller, the law clerk in Dickens's *The Old Curiosity Shop*, has a clear perception about the danger of family quarrels. His words remind us to work toward a peaceful resolution. Has a family quarrel come between you and someone you love? Then take it to God in prayer, and ask Him to show you a way to resolve it. God can take "a devil" of a situation and change it into something good.

✣

STARTING A QUARREL IS LIKE BREACHING A DAM;
SO DROP THE MATTER BEFORE A DISPUTE BREAKS OUT.

Proverbs 17:14 NIV

PERFECT LOVE

The spinster aunt took up a large watering-pot which lay in one corner, and was about to leave the arbour. Mr. Tupman detained her and drew her to a seat beside him. "Miss Wardle!" said he. . . .

"Miss Wardle," said Mr. Tupman, "you are an angel."

"Mr. Tupman!" exclaimed Rachael, blushing as red as the watering-pot itself.

"Nay," said the eloquent Pickwickian—"I know it but too well."

"All women are angels, they say," murmured the lady playfully.

"Then what can you be; or to what, without presumption, can I compare you?" replied Mr. Tupman. "Where was the woman ever seen who resembled you? Where else could I hope to find so rare a combination of excellence and beauty? . . ." Here Mr. Tupman paused . . .

The lady turned aside her head. "Men are such deceivers," she softly whispered.

"They are, they are," ejaculated Mr. Tupman; "but not all men. There lives at least one being who can never change—one being who would be content to devote his whole existence to your happiness—who lives but in your eyes—who breathes but in your smiles—who bears the heavy burden of life itself only for you."

"Could such an individual be found—" said the lady.

"But he CAN be found," said the ardent Mr. Tupman, interposing. "He IS found. He is here, Miss Wardle."

—The Pickwick Papers

The womanizing Mr. Tupman wooed Rachael Wardle by vowing to live only for her and never change. The observant Rachael wondered: *Could such an individual exist?*

The answer is yes, but not in the person of Mr. Tupman. The only love that endures forever is God's love (Psalm 136:26). He is the One who bears our burdens daily (Psalm 68:19). God does not change like shifting shadows (James 1:17). Not only does God love us, but God *is* love (1 John 4:8). In fact, the only reason that we are able to love at all is because God first loved us (1 John 4:19).

As a human, Mr. Tupman could not guarantee that his love for Miss Wardle would never change. Only God's love is guaranteed. The covenant of His devotion is this: God loves us so much that He gave His one and only Son, that whoever believes in Him shall not perish but have eternal life (John 3:16). That is perfect love. Although we are all sinners and not worthy of heaven, God still loves us and wants us to be with Him and loved by Him forever. When you tell someone that you love him or her, remember the commitment that God makes to you with His love, and then honor Him with yours.

✤

NOTHING CAN EVER SEPARATE US FROM GOD'S LOVE.

Romans 8:38 NLT

THE ENEMY

It was a chill, damp, windy night, when . . . [he] emerged from his den. He . . . slunk down the street as quickly as he could . . .

The mud lay thick upon the stones, and a black mist hung over the streets; the rain fell sluggishly down, and everything felt cold and clammy to the touch. . . . As he glided stealthily along, creeping beneath the shelter of the walls and doorways, the hideous old man seemed like some loathsome reptile, engendered in the slime and darkness through which he moved: crawling forth, by night, in search of some rich offal for a meal.

He kept on his course, through many winding and narrow ways, until he reached Bethnal Green; then, turning suddenly off to the left, he soon became involved in a maze of the mean and dirty streets which abound in that close and densely-populated quarter.

[He] was evidently too familiar with the ground he traversed to be at all bewildered, either by the darkness of the night, or the intricacies of the way. He hurried through several alleys and streets, and at length turned into one, lighted only by a single lamp . . . At the door of a house . . . he knocked; having exchanged a few muttered words with the person who opened it, he walked upstairs.

A dog growled as he touched the handle of a room-door; and a man's voice demanded who was there.

—Oliver Twist

ickens paints a gloomy picture in this scene from *Oliver Twist*. One can almost hear the footsteps of the hideous old man as he prowls London's dark streets and alleys.

Satan travels like this, gliding stealthily along, crawling through the winding ways of the world. The book of Genesis tells of his encounter with Eve in the garden of Eden: "Now the serpent was more crafty than any other beast of the field . . . He said to the woman, 'Did God actually say, "You shall not eat of any tree in the garden"?' And the woman said . . . 'We may eat of the fruit of the trees in the garden, but God said, "You shall not eat of the fruit of the tree that is in the midst of the garden, neither shall you touch it, lest you die."' But the serpent said . . . , 'You will not surely die. For God knows that when you eat of it your eyes will be opened, and you will be like God, knowing good and evil'" (Genesis 3:1–5 ESV).

Paul warned us to be watchful of Satan's trickery: "For our struggle is not against flesh and blood, but against . . . the powers of this dark world and against the spiritual forces of evil" (Ephesians 6:12 NIV). At times when you feel torn between right and wrong, remember the hideous old man from *Oliver Twist*. "Resist the devil, and he will flee from you" (James 4:7 NIV).

☩

"AND DO NOT LEAD US INTO TEMPTATION, BUT
DELIVER US FROM THE EVIL ONE."

Matthew 6:13

GOD'S ARMY

"Master," he replied, "I am Nobody, and little likely to be heard of (nor yet much wanted to be heard of, perhaps), except when there is some trouble. But it never begins with me, and it never can end with me. As sure as Death, it comes down to me, and it goes up from me." . . .

So Nobody lived and died in the old, old, old way; and this, in the main, is the whole of Nobody's story.

Had he no name, you ask? . . . It matters little what his name was . . .

If you were ever in the Belgian villages near the field of Waterloo, you will have seen, in some quiet little church, a monument erected by faithful companions in arms to the memory of Colonel A, Major B, Captains C, D and E, Lieutenants F and G, Ensigns H, I and J, seven non-commissioned officers, and one hundred and thirty rank and file, who fell in the discharge of their duty on the memorable day. The story of Nobody is the story of the rank and file of the earth. They bear their share of the battle; they have their part in the victory; they fall; they leave no name but in the mass. The march of the proudest of us, leads to the dusty way by which they go. O! Let us think of them this year . . . and not forget them.

—"Nobody's Story"

Nobody's Story" is one of Dickens's lesser-known works. Although it was published as a Christmas story, there was little Christmas spirit in this tale of Nobody, a man who embodied the overburdened poor in London. Nevertheless, this passage from the story can remind us of the Christian "soldiers" who give their all for Christ, anonymously.

In Ephesians 6, the apostle Paul gives these instructions to Christians fighting for righteousness: "Put on the whole armor of God, that you may be able to stand against the wiles of the devil. For we do not wrestle against flesh and blood, but against principalities, against powers, against the rulers of the darkness of this age, against spiritual hosts of wickedness in the heavenly places. Therefore take up the whole armor of God, that you may be able to withstand in the evil day, and having done all, to stand. Stand therefore, having girded your waist with truth, having put on the breastplate of righteousness, and having shod your feet with the preparation of the gospel of peace; above all, taking the shield of faith with which you will be able to quench all the fiery darts of the wicked one. And take the helmet of salvation, and the sword of the Spirit, which is the word of God" (vv. 11–17).

Today, there are countless Christians serving in Christ's Army around the world. They minister in many ways to combat evil and win souls for Christ. And athough they may seem invisible to those of this world, their heavenly Father knows them, loves them, and calls them by name. For those who choose to serve in the Lord's Army are the purchased children of the King.

✣

FIGHT THE GOOD FIGHT OF FAITH.

1 Timothy 6:12

DREAMS

The cold, feeble dawn of a January morning was stealing in at the windows of the common sleeping-room, when Nicholas, raising himself on his arm, looked among the prostrate forms which on every side surrounded him, as though in search of some particular object. . . .

As they lay closely packed together, covered, for warmth's sake, . . . little could be distinguished but the sharp outlines of pale faces . . . There were some who, lying on their backs with upturned faces and clenched hands, just visible in the leaden light, bore more the aspect of dead bodies than of living creatures; and there were others coiled up into strange and fantastic postures, such as might have been taken for the uneasy efforts of pain to gain some temporary relief, rather than the freaks of slumber. A few—and these were among the youngest of the children—slept peacefully on, with smiles upon their faces, dreaming perhaps of home; but ever and again a deep and heavy sigh, breaking the stillness of the room, announced that some new sleeper had awakened to . . . another day; and, as morning took the place of night, the smiles gradually faded away, with the friendly darkness which had given them birth.

Dreams are the bright creatures of poem and legend, who sport on earth in the night season, and melt away in the first beam of the sun, which lights grim care and stern reality on their daily pilgrimage through the world.

—The Life and Adventures of Nicholas Nickleby

In this passage, Dickens portrays dreams as things that "melt away in the first beam of the sun." But our dreams do not have to end at sunrise. Harriet Tubman, a former slave turned abolitionist, said, "Every great dream begins with a dreamer. Always remember, you have within you the strength, the patience, and the passion to reach for the stars to change the world."

The Bible tells the story of a dreamer named Joseph. He was a teenager, the youngest of his siblings, when he had a dream. Joseph told his brothers. "We were binding sheaves of grain out in the field when suddenly my sheaf rose and stood upright, while your sheaves gathered around mine and bowed down to it" (Genesis 37:6–7 NIV). Joseph's brothers did not like the idea of bowing to their younger brother. They hated Joseph for his dream, and they sold him into slavery. Still, Joseph believed that God had something great in store for him. After many trials and much patience, Joseph's dream came true—he became the chief minister (governor) of Egypt (Genesis 41:41–46).

God has a plan for each of us. Often He instills dreams—ambitions—in our hearts and encourages us to reach for them. And whatever dream God puts into your heart, you can trust Him to lead you to it.

✠

O LORD, I KNOW THE WAY OF MAN IS NOT IN HIMSELF;
IT IS NOT IN MAN WHO WALKS TO DIRECT HIS OWN STEPS.

Jeremiah 10:23

ONE FAMILY

The reader must not expect to know where I live. At present, it is true, my abode may be a question of little or no import to anybody; but if I should carry my readers with me, as I hope to do, and there should spring up between them and me feelings of homely affection and regard attaching something of interest to matters ever so slightly connected with my fortunes or my speculations, even my place of residence might one day have a kind of charm for them. . . .

I am not a churlish old man. Friendless I can never be, for all mankind are my kindred, and I am on ill terms with no one member of my great family. But for many years I have led a lonely, solitary life;—what wound I sought to heal, what sorrow to forget, originally, matters not now; it is sufficient that retirement has become a habit with me, and that I am unwilling to break the spell which for so long a time has shed its quiet influence upon my home and heart.

I live in a venerable suburb of London, in an old house which in bygone days was a famous resort for merry roysterers . . . It is a silent, shady place, with a paved courtyard so full of echoes, that sometimes I am tempted to believe that faint responses to the noises of old times linger there.

—Master Humphrey's Clock

ickens's character Master Humphrey lived a solitary life surrounded by a small circle of friends. Still, in his advancing years, he did not see himself as grumpy and boorish. He felt at peace with his quiet life, believing that all mankind was his family. How, one might wonder, could a lonely man like Master Humphrey be content?

Galatians 3 teaches that we become members of God's family through faith in Jesus Christ. It says, "You are all sons of God through faith in Christ Jesus . . . There is neither Jew nor Greek, slave nor free, male nor female, for you are all one in Christ Jesus" (vv. 26–28 NIV). We are one in Christ, having all been created by the same God. We are God's sons and daughters when we believe in Jesus and have faith in Him. John 1:12 confirms this: "Yet to all who received [Jesus], to those who believed in his name, he gave the right to become children of God" (NIV).

As children of God, we need not be lonely, because God and our Christian brothers and sisters surround us. Master Humphrey said that he was on good terms with all in his "great family." This is how we find contentment. As God's children, we love one another. And in doing so, we show that we are followers of Christ (John 13:34–35).

⚜

I WILL BE A FATHER TO YOU, AND YOU SHALL BE MY
SONS AND DAUGHTERS, SAYS THE LORD ALMIGHTY.

2 Corinthians 6:18

REGARDING HANDS

He knocked softly, with his hook, at Florence's door, twice or thrice; but, receiving no answer, ventured first to peep in, and then to enter: emboldened to take the latter step, perhaps, by the familiar recognition of Diogenes, who, stretched upon the ground by the side of her couch, wagged his tail, and winked his eyes at the Captain, without being at the trouble of getting up.

She was sleeping heavily, and moaning in her sleep; and Captain Cuttle, with a perfect awe of her youth, and beauty, and her sorrow, raised her head, and adjusted the coat that covered her, where it had fallen off, and darkened the window a little more that she might sleep on, and crept out again, and took his post of watch upon the stairs. All this, with a touch and tread as light as Florence's own.

Long may it remain in this mixed world a point not easy of decision, which is the more beautiful evidence of the Almighty's goodness—the delicate fingers that are formed for sensitiveness and sympathy of touch, and made to minister to pain and grief, or the rough hard Captain Cuttle hand, that the heart teaches, guides, and softens in a moment!

Florence slept upon her couch, forgetful of her homelessness and orphanage, and Captain Cuttle watched upon the stairs. A louder sob or moan than usual, brought him sometimes to her door; but by degrees she slept more peacefully, and the Captain's watch was undisturbed.

—Dombey and Son

ickens presents a soft image of contrast and affection in this passage from *Dombey and Son*. Crusty Captain Cuttle, his missing right hand replaced by a sturdy hook, knocks softly at Florence's door. Upon entering her room, the captain uses his strong left hand to cover the sleeping girl with a coat that had fallen away. He takes care that his touch is gentle so not to wake her.

In the Bible, the Lord told Jeremiah to go to the potter's house. There, Jeremiah saw the potter at work at his potter's wheel. The pot he was working on was misshapen, and as Jeremiah watched, the potter reworked the clay with his hands, gently molding it into a better pot. Then, the Lord said to Jeremiah, "Can I not do with you as this potter does? . . . Like clay in the hand of the potter, so are you in my hand" (Jeremiah 18:1–6 NIV).

God's hands are gentle, yet powerfully built. Psalm 89 praises Him, saying, "Your arm is endued with power; your hand is strong" (v. 13 NIV). "In his hand are the depths of the earth, and the mountain peaks belong to him" (Psalm 95:4 NIV). Even "the skies proclaim the works of his hands" (Psalm 19:1 NIV). Today, and every day, God holds you gently in His hands. He shapes you as a potter shapes his clay, determined to make you the best you can be.

✠

SEE, I HAVE INSCRIBED YOU ON THE PALMS OF MY HANDS.

Isaiah 49:16

IDOLATRY

Mr. Smallweed's grandfather . . . is in a helpless condition as to his lower, and nearly so as to his upper, limbs, but his mind is unimpaired. It holds, as well as it ever held, the first four rules of arithmetic and a certain small collection of the hardest facts. In respect of ideality, reverence, wonder, and other such phrenological attributes, it is no worse off than it used to be. Everything that Mr. Smallweed's grandfather ever put away in his mind was a grub at first, and is a grub at last. In all his life he has never bred a single butterfly.

The father of this pleasant grandfather, of the neighbourhood of Mount Pleasant, was a horny-skinned, two-legged, money-getting species of spider who spun webs to catch unwary flies and retired into holes until they were entrapped. The name of this old pagan's god was Compound Interest. He lived for it, married it, died of it. Meeting with a heavy loss in an honest little enterprise in which all the loss was intended to have been on the other side, he broke something—something necessary to his existence, therefore it couldn't have been his heart—and made an end of his career. As his character was not good, and he had been bred at a charity school in a complete course, according to question and answer, of those ancient people the Amorites and Hittites, he was frequently quoted as an example of the failure of education.

—*Bleak House*

In this passage, Charles Dickens makes reference to pagan idol worship. First, he calls Mr. Smallweed a pagan who bows down to the god of compound interest. Then he says that Mr. Smallweed learned from the example of the Amorites and Hittites—pagan dwellers of the land of Canaan in Abraham's time.

God is very clear that He is the One and Only God. His First Commandment says: "You shall have no other gods before me. You shall not make for yourself an image in the form of anything in heaven above or on the earth beneath or in the waters below. You shall not bow down to them or worship them; for I, the LORD your God, am a jealous God, punishing the children for the sin of the parents to the third and fourth generation of those who hate me, but showing love to a thousand generations of those who love me and keep my commandments" (Exodus 20:3-6 NIV).

When we think of idols, we might recall the Israelites transgression when they bowed down to a golden calf (Exodus 32), but an idol is anything that becomes more important to us than God: money, success, technology, leisure. These things are God's gifts to us, but when we assign them undue importance, they become idols. The good news is that when we make God the center of everything we do, He is the only God we need.

✠

I, EVEN I, AM HE, AND THERE IS NO GOD BESIDES ME.

Deuteronomy 32:39

HERE AND NOW

I paid my fee of twopence upon entering, to one of the money-changers who sit within the Temple; and falling . . . into the quiet train of thought which such a place awakens, paced the echoing stones like some old monk whose present world lay all within its walls. . . . I began to ascend, almost unconsciously, the flight of steps leading to the several wonders of the building, and found myself before a barrier where another money-taker sat, who demanded which among them I would choose to see. There were the stone gallery, he said, and the whispering gallery, the geometrical staircase, the room of models, the clock . . . I stopped him there, and chose that sight from all the rest.

I groped my way into the Turret which it occupies, and saw before me, in a kind of loft, what seemed to be a great, old oaken press with folding doors. These being thrown back by the attendant . . . disclosed a complicated crowd of wheels and chains in iron and brass,—great, sturdy, rattling engines, . . . and these were the Clock! Its very pulse . . . was like no other clock. It did not mark the flight of every moment with a gentle second stroke, as though it would check old Time, and have him stay his pace in pity, but measured it with one sledge-hammer beat, as if its business were to crush the seconds as they came trooping on, and remorselessly to clear a path before the Day of Judgment.

—Master Humphrey's Clock

Mr. Humphrey perceived the clock, and time itself, as something powerful that with its every "sledge-hammer beat" crushed the present and led mankind marching toward the future. The prominent Scottish pastor and teacher Oswald Chambers had another observation of time. He focused on the present. Chambers said, "I have to get to the point of the absolute and unquestionable relationship that takes everything exactly as it comes from Him. God never guides us at some time in the future, but always here and now. Realize that the Lord is here now, and the freedom you receive is immediate."[1]

Psalm 139:7–10 reminds us that God is always with us: "Where can I go from Your Spirit? Or where can I flee from Your presence? If I ascend into heaven, You are there; If I make my bed in hell, behold, You are there. If I take the wings of the morning, and dwell in the uttermost parts of the sea, even there Your hand shall lead me, and Your right hand shall hold me."

Notice that these scripture verses are written in the present tense. God is not only in heaven, waiting for us there, but, as Oswald Chambers said, He is here and now. God is in every beat of the clock, guiding our daily steps with His never-ending devotion and love.

☩

I AM WITH YOU ALWAYS, EVEN TO THE END OF THE AGE.

Matthew 28:20

SELF-CONFIDENCE

Dear Mr. Clennam, . . .

I am now going to devote an hour to writing to you again. This time, I write from Rome. . . .

I ought now to mention Mr. Gowan, before I say what little . . . I have to say about [his wife]. He must admire her beauty, and he must be proud of her, for everybody praises it, and he must be fond of her, and I do not doubt that he is—but in his way. You know his way, and if it appears as careless and discontented in your eyes as it does in mine, I am not wrong in thinking that it might be better suited to her. If it does not seem so to you, I am quite sure I am wholly mistaken; for your unchanged poor child confides in your knowledge and goodness more than she could ever tell you if she was to try. But don't be frightened, I am not going to try. Owing (as I think, if you think so too) to Mr. Gowan's unsettled and dissatisfied way, he applies himself to his profession very little.

He does nothing steadily or patiently; but equally takes things up and throws them down, and does them, or leaves them undone, without caring about them. When I have heard him talking to Papa during the sittings for the picture, I have sat wondering whether it could be that he has no belief in anybody else, because he has no belief in himself.

—Little Dorrit

This passage, taken from a letter written by twenty-something Amy Dorrit to her older friend Arthur Clennam, describes the not-so-nice painter Mr. Gowen. Amy wonders whether his careless and ill-tempered attitude might come from a lack of self-confidence.

Self-confidence is defined by *Merriam-Webster's Dictionary* as "confidence in oneself and in one's powers and abilities." But how confident can we be when we rely only on ourselves? The Bible says, "For the LORD will be your confidence" (Proverbs 3:26), and "Such confidence as this is ours through Christ before God. Not that we are competent in ourselves to claim anything for ourselves, but our competence comes from God" (2 Corinthians 3:4–5 NIV).

In 1 Samuel 17, we find the story of David, a slight, young man courageously fighting Goliath, a bullish, nine-foot-tall warrior from Gath. David finds his confidence in trusting in the Lord, and armed with just a slingshot and stones, he defeats the giant soldier. Could he have done this by himself? No!

Our own powers and abilities sometimes fail us, but there is One who never fails. The story of David illustrates that true self-confidence is dependent upon a solid trust in God. When we rely on God, His confidence flows through us. We are then able to behave in a Christlike way rather than withdrawing or acting out, like the irascible Mr. Gowen.

✣

BUT BLESSED IS THE ONE WHO TRUSTS IN THE LORD,
WHOSE CONFIDENCE IS IN HIM.

Jeremiah 17:7 NIV

Concerning Debt

They passed through the inner gate, and descended a short flight of steps. The key was turned after them; and Mr. Pickwick found himself, for the first time in his life, within the walls of a debtors' prison.

Mr. Tom Roker, the gentleman who had accompanied Mr. Pickwick into the prison, turned sharp round to the right when he got to the bottom of the little flight of steps, and led the way, through an iron gate which stood open, and up another short flight of steps, into a long narrow gallery, dirty and low, paved with stone, and very dimly lighted by a window at each remote end.

"This," said the gentleman, thrusting his hands into his pockets, and looking carelessly over his shoulder to Mr. Pickwick—"this here is the hall flight."

"Oh," replied Mr. Pickwick, looking down a dark and filthy staircase, which appeared to lead to a range of damp and gloomy stone vaults, beneath the ground, "and those, I suppose, are the little cellars where the prisoners keep their small quantities of coals. Unpleasant places to have to go down to, but very convenient, I dare say."

"Yes, I shouldn't wonder if they was convenient," replied the gentleman, "seeing that . . . people live there . . ."

"My friend," said Mr. Pickwick, "you don't really mean to say that human beings live down in those wretched dungeons?" . . .

"Live down there! Yes, and die down there, too very often!" replied Mr. Roker.

—*The Pickwick Papers*

When Mr. Pickwick's landlady sued him and won, Pickwick chose to go to a London debtor's prison rather than falsely admit his guilt. In Dickens's time, citizens who could not pay their debts were confined to prisons. Dickens's father was in a debtor's prison when Charles went to work at a boot polish factory to help support his mother and siblings. These childhood events inspired Charles Dickens to write about the poor and the inhumanity of the London prison system in his novels.

Poverty in itself is not a sin, but the Bible clearly states that Christians should not live beyond their means and build up debt. "Give to everyone what you owe them: If you owe taxes, pay taxes; if revenue, then revenue; if respect, then respect; if honor, then honor. Let no debt remain outstanding, except the continuing debt to love one another" (Romans 13:7–8 NIV).

We live in a time where credit is a way of life. Debtor prisons no longer exist, but we can become imprisoned in a lifetime of bills, high interest rates, and late fees. God wants us to be debt free. As we work toward that goal, He "will meet all [our] needs according to his glorious riches in Christ Jesus" (Philippians 4:19 NIV). And indeed, He has already met our greatest need—the forgiveness of the vast debt of our sins through the death of His own Son, Jesus Christ.

⚜

FORGIVE US OUR DEBTS.

Matthew 6:12

ASKING FOR HELP

The King then sighed so heavily, and seemed so low-spirited, and sat down so miserably, leaning his head upon his hand, and his elbow upon the kitchen table pushed away in the corner, that the seventeen Princes and Princesses crept softly out of the kitchen, and left him alone with the Princess Alicia and the angelic baby.

"What is the matter, Papa?"

"I am dreadfully poor, my child."

"Have you no money at all, Papa?"

"None my child."

"Is there no way left of getting any, Papa?"

"No way," said the King. "I have tried very hard, and I have tried all ways."

When she heard those last words, the Princess Alicia began to put her hand into the pocket where she kept the magic fish-bone.

"Papa," said she, "when we have tried very hard, and tried all ways, we must have done our very very best?"

"No doubt, Alicia."

"When we have done our very very best, Papa, and that is not enough, then I think the right time must have come for asking help of others." This was the very secret connected with the magic fish-bone. . . .

So she took out of her pocket the magic fish-bone that had been dried and rubbed and polished till it shone like mother-of-pearl; and she gave it one little kiss and wished it was quarter day.

—"The Magic Fishbone"

The Magic Fishbone" is one of four stories Dickens wrote in his novella *A Holiday Romance*. Unlike his other works, this fairy tale was written for children and in the voice of a child. It tells the story of a king determined to solve his problem completely on his own, without help from anyone.

And how often do we ourselves do the same thing? But the simple truth is this: even when we do our best, we sometimes need help. Too often it is our pride that prevents our seeking that help. Proverbs 16:18 offers this bit of wisdom: "Pride goes before destruction, a haughty spirit before a fall" (NIV). There is no shame in asking for help, particularly when asking of the Lord. The Bible says in Matthew 7:7, "Ask and it will be given to you; seek and you will find; knock and the door will be opened to you" (NIV).

An "I can do it all by myself" attitude separates us from God. Our best help—help we can surely count on—comes from Him. Perhaps you remember these words from Psalm 121: "I lift up my eyes to the hills—where does my help come from? My help comes from the LORD, the Maker of heaven and earth. He will not let your foot slip—he who watches over you will not slumber" (vv. 1–4 NIV). When we let go of our pride and ask God for help, we can trust that He will provide exactly what we need.

✛

UNLESS THE LORD HAD BEEN MY HELP,
MY SOUL WOULD SOON HAVE SETTLED IN SILENCE.

Psalm 94:17

HEAVENLY WISDOM

Louisa turned upon her pillow . . . She turned her head back . . . and lay with her face towards the door, until it opened and her father entered. . . .

"My dear Louisa. My poor daughter. My unfortunate child." . . . He took her outstretched hand, and retained it in his.

"My dear, I have remained all night at my table, pondering again and again on what has so painfully passed between us. When I consider your character; when I consider that what has been known to me for hours, has been concealed by you for years; when I consider under what immediate pressure it has been forced from you at last; I come to the conclusion that I cannot but mistrust myself." . . .

She had turned upon her pillow, and lay with her face upon her arm, so that he could not see it. All her wildness and passion had subsided; but, though softened, she was not in tears. . . .

"Some persons hold," he pursued . . . hesitating, "that there is a wisdom of the Head, and that there is a wisdom of the Heart. I have not supposed so; but, as I have said, I mistrust myself now. I have supposed the head to be all-sufficient. It may not be all-sufficient; how can I venture this morning to say it is! If that other kind of wisdom should be what I have neglected, and should be the instinct that is wanted, Louisa—"

He suggested it very doubtfully, as if he were half unwilling to admit it even now.

—Hard Times

This scene from Dickens's *Hard Times* comes on the heels of Louisa Gradgrind complaining to her father, Thomas, about his lack of parenting skills. (A similar scene repeats, in one form or another, in many homes today.) Thomas, a mathematician who deals in absolutes and certainties, wonders whether wisdom of the head is sufficient, or if it should be tempered by wisdom of the heart. But whether our wisdom comes from the heart or the head, if it is not steeped in God's wisdom, it will always be insufficient.

The Bible says this about human wisdom: "For the wisdom of this world is foolishness with God" (1 Corinthians 1:19). Rather than following our own notions, we should seek to fill our hearts with godly wisdom. For we are promised, "If any of you lacks wisdom, let him ask of God, who gives to all liberally and without reproach, and it will be given to him" (James 1:5). In the search for wisdom, the father in Proverbs 2 advises, "If you accept my words and store up my commands within you, turning your ear to wisdom and applying your heart to understanding . . . and if you look for it as for silver and search for it as for hidden treasure, then you will understand the fear of the LORD and find the knowledge of God. For the LORD gives wisdom; and from his mouth come knowledge and understanding" (vv. 1–6 NIV).

Human wisdom alone—no matter how well thought out—is not sufficient, "But the wisdom that comes from heaven is first of all pure; then peace-loving, considerate, submissive, full of mercy and good fruit, impartial and sincere" (James 3:17 NIV). It is this that we should seek.

✠

HAPPY IS THE MAN WHO FINDS WISDOM,
AND THE MAN WHO GAINS UNDERSTANDING.

Proverbs 3:13

ABOUT PERSPECTIVE

"A merry Christmas, Bob!" said Scrooge, with an earnestness that could not be mistaken . . . "A merrier Christmas, Bob, my good fellow, than I have given you, for many a year! I'll raise your salary, and endeavour to assist your struggling family . . . !"

Scrooge was better than his word. He did it all, and infinitely more; and to Tiny Tim, who did *NOT* die, he was a second father. He became as good a friend . . . and as good a man, as the good old city knew, or any other good old city, town, or borough, in the good old world. Some people laughed to see the alteration in him, but he let them laugh, and little heeded them; for he was wise enough to know that nothing ever happened on this globe, for good, at which some people did not have their fill of laughter in the outset; and knowing that such as these would be blind anyway, he thought it quite as well that they should wrinkle up their eyes in grins, as have the malady in less attractive forms. His own heart laughed: and that was quite enough for him.

He had no further intercourse with Spirits . . . and it was always said of him, that he knew how to keep Christmas well, if any man alive possessed the knowledge. May that be truly said of us, and all of us! And so, as Tiny Tim observed, God bless Us, Every One!

—*A Christmas Carol*

Three spirits visited Scrooge and accompanied him on a journey through his past, present, and future. After seeing how dismal the end would be for him, Scrooge changed his ways and vowed to always "keep Christmas well." Dickens assures us that the old gentleman kept his promise. You might say that Scrooge had a change of perspective.

Jesus taught about perspective in the Beatitudes. He said, "Blessed are the poor in spirit, for theirs is the kingdom of heaven. Blessed are those who mourn, for they shall be comforted. Blessed are the meek, for they shall inherit the earth. Blessed are those who hunger and thirst for righteousness, for they shall be filled. Blessed are the merciful, for they shall obtain mercy. Blessed are the pure in heart, for they shall see God. Blessed are the peacemakers, for they shall be called sons of God. Blessed are those who are persecuted for righteousness' sake, for theirs is the kingdom of heaven" (Matthew 5:3–10).

We have a choice about the way we view the events of our lives. Our goal as Christians should be the view that God is in all circumstances. The apostle Paul had that kind of heavenly perspective. Even during his trials—a shipwreck, persecution, imprisonment—he wrote about the joy that came from his faith. Choosing to have a heavenly perspective can make all the difference in life.

⚜

A MERRY HEART MAKES A CHEERFUL COUNTENANCE.

Proverbs 15:13

VALLEYS

I came, one evening before sunset, down into a valley . . . In the course of my descent to it, by the winding track along the mountain-side, from which I saw it shining far below, I think some long-unwonted sense of beauty and tranquillity, some softening influence awakened by its peace, moved faintly in my breast. I remember pausing once, with a kind of sorrow that was not all oppressive, not quite despairing. I remember almost hoping that some better change was possible within me.

I came into the valley, as the evening sun was shining on the remote heights of snow, that closed it in, like eternal clouds. The bases of the mountains forming the gorge in which the little village lay, were richly green; and high above this gentler vegetation, grew forests of dark fir . . . Above these, were range upon range of craggy steeps . . . and smooth verdure-specks of pasture, all gradually blending with the crowning snow. Dotted here and there on the mountain's-side, each tiny dot a home, were lonely wooden cottages, so dwarfed by the towering heights that they appeared too small for toys. So did even the clustered village in the valley, with its wooden bridge across the stream, where the stream tumbled over broken rocks, and roared away among the trees. In the quiet air, there was a sound of distant singing—shepherd voices; but, as one bright evening cloud floated midway along the mountain's-side, I could almost have believed it came from there, and was not earthly music.

—David Copperfield

In poetic prose, Dickens describes the immensity of this valley in which David Copperfield walks while grieving his wife, Dora's, death. Dickens hints, ever so subtly, that Someone unseen walks there with David.

When we think about the valleys in our lives, we may remember the words of Psalm 23: "Yea, though I walk through the valley of the shadow of death, I will fear no evil: for thou art with me; thy rod and thy staff they comfort me" (v. 4 KJV). When John the Baptist preached about the coming of our Lord, he echoed the words found in Isaiah 40:4. He said, "Prepare the way of the LORD; make His paths straight. Every valley shall be filled and every mountain and hill brought low; the crooked places shall be made straight and the rough ways smooth; and all flesh shall see the salvation of God" (Luke 3:4–6). Psalm 104:10 reminds us that "[God] sends springs into the valleys; they flow among the hills."

Whenever we find ourselves in one of life's valleys, we can take heart that God is with us every step of the way. He hears us when we pray, He creates a pathway for us to walk upon, and He guides our footsteps. When we put our faith in Him, our valleys fill with His compassionate presence.

✣

I AM THE ROSE OF SHARON, AND THE LILY OF THE VALLEYS.

Song of Solomon 2:1

GIVING OUR BEST

I have been very fortunate in worldly matters; many men have worked much harder, and not succeeded half so well; but I never could have done what I have done, without the habits of punctuality, order, and diligence, without the determination to concentrate myself on one object at a time, no matter how quickly its successor should come upon its heels, . . . I do not hold one natural gift, I dare say, that I have not abused. My meaning simply is, that whatever I have tried to do in life, I have tried with all my heart to do well; that whatever I have devoted myself to, I have devoted myself to completely; that in great aims and in small, I have always been thoroughly in earnest. I have never believed it possible that any natural or improved ability can claim immunity from the companionship of the steady, plain, hard-working qualities, and hope to gain its end. There is no such thing as such fulfilment on this earth. Some happy talent, and some fortunate opportunity, may form the two sides of the ladder on which some men mount, but the rounds of that ladder must be made of stuff to stand wear and tear; and there is no substitute for thorough-going, ardent, and sincere earnestness. Never to put one hand to anything, on which I could throw my whole self; and never to affect depreciation of my work, whatever it was; I find, now, to have been my golden rules.

—David Copperfield

In this scene, Dickens shows us that David Copperfield has grown into a successful man. David credits his success to an unwavering commitment to do his best. He tackles his work in earnest. On "earnestness" Charles Spurgeon wrote: "The church will only get right by each man getting right. Oh, that we might get back into an earnest zeal for our Lord's love and service." God wants us to live right and, like David Copperfield, to give our best at whatever we do.

In his letter to the Colossians, the apostle Paul said, "Whatever you do, work at it with all your heart, as working for the Lord, not for men. . . . It is the Lord Christ you are serving" (3:23–24 NIV). And about success, Paul continued, "You do well in everything . . . You do well in faith and in speaking. You do well in knowledge and complete commitment. . . . So make sure that you also do well in the grace of giving to others" (2 Corinthians 8:7 NIRV).

Jesus is our model for giving our best. Everything He did was in earnest and for us, especially when He died on the cross for our sins. Because of this, no sacrifice should be too great for us to make for Him. Whatever we do, we should do it well to honor the Lord.

✢

WHATEVER YOUR HAND FINDS TO DO,
DO IT WITH YOUR MIGHT.

Ecclesiastes 9:10

TOWARD HEAVEN

Mr. Meagles, Doyce, and Clennam, without speaking, walked up and down on the brink of the river, in the light of the rising moon, for a few minutes; and then Doyce lingered behind, and went into the house. Mr. Meagles and Clennam walked up and down together for a few minutes more without speaking, until at length the former broke silence. . . .

"Will you come in?" said Mr. Meagles . . .

"In a little while."

Mr. Meagles fell away, and [Clennam] was left alone. When he had walked on the river's brink in the peaceful moonlight for some half an hour, he put his hand in his breast and tenderly took out the handful of roses. Perhaps he put them to his heart, perhaps he put them to his lips, but certainly he bent down on the shore and gently launched them on the flowing river. Pale and unreal in the moonlight, the river floated them away. The lights were bright within doors when he entered, and the faces on which they shone, his own face not excepted, were soon quietly cheerful. They talked of many subjects (his partner never had had such a ready store to draw upon for the beguiling of the time), and so to bed, and to sleep. While the flowers, pale and unreal in the moonlight, floated away upon the river; and thus do greater things that once were in our breasts, and near our hearts, flow from us to the eternal seas.

—Little Dorrit

aying good-bye to someone, or something, we love is not easy. In this scene from his novel *Little Dorrit*, Dickens paints a vivid image of what it means to say good-bye. Mr. Clennam left roses in memory of a loved one, and as they flow to the eternal seas, so do we Christians drift toward eternal life.

Jesus encourages us to always look toward the eternal life of heaven. The Bible says that eternal life is God's gift to us (Romans 6:23). The only way to heaven is through Jesus. He tells us, "I am the door. If anyone enters by Me, he will be saved" (John 10:9). Although saying good-bye at the death of a loved one is a sorrowful thing, 1 Corinthians 15:22 holds this promise: "For as in Adam all die, even so in Christ all shall be made alive."

Looking toward heaven is more than the vision of a futuristic blessing. It is the present confidence that when we say good-bye to someone on Earth, it is only for a season. After Jesus' friend Lazarus died, Jesus said to his sister Martha: "I am the resurrection and the life. He who believes in Me . . . shall never die." Then he asked Martha a question that each of us should ponder: "Do you believe this?" (John 11:25–26).

✠

AND I WILL DWELL IN THE HOUSE OF THE LORD FOREVER.

Psalm 23:6

On Comfort

In the exhaustless catalogue of Heaven's mercies to mankind, the power we have of finding some germs of comfort in the hardest trials must ever occupy the foremost place; not only because it supports and upholds us when we most require to be sustained, but because in this source of consolation there is something, we have reason to believe, of the divine spirit; something of that goodness which detects amidst our own evil doings, a redeeming quality; something which, even in our fallen nature, we possess in common with the angels; which had its being in the old time when they trod the earth, and lingers on it yet, in pity.

How often, on their journey, did the widow remember with a grateful heart, that out of his deprivation Barnaby's cheerfulness and affection sprung! How often did she call to mind that but for that, he might have been sullen, morose, unkind, far removed from her—vicious, perhaps, and cruel! How often had she cause for comfort, in his strength, and hope, and in his simple nature! . . . The world to him was full of happiness; in every tree, and plant, and flower, in every bird, and beast, and tiny insect whom a breath of summer wind laid low upon the ground, he had delight. His delight was hers; and where many a wise son would have made her sorrowful, this poor [child] filled her breast with thankfulness and love.

—Barnaby Rudge

harles Dickens understood the value of providing comfort. In his novel *Barnaby Rudge*, he ascribed its source as God—the Divine Spirit—and urged readers to search for bits of comfort even in their most difficult trials. This he illustrated when the widow Rudge found comfort in the simple nature of Barnaby, her mentally challenged son.

The apostle Paul praised God for His comforting ways and taught that the comforting nature of God is our example for bringing consolation to others. He wrote, "Praise be to the God and Father of our Lord Jesus Christ, the Father of compassion and the God of all comfort, who comforts us in all our troubles, so that we can comfort those in any trouble with the comfort we ourselves have received from God" (2 Corinthians 1:3–4 NIV). Think on those words "the Father of compassion and the God of all comfort."

True comfort comes from our heavenly Father. By studying the ways He comforts us, we can learn to be more like Him. We provide comfort through reassurance, encouragement, and sharing our faith. Does a friend in your life need comforting? Think about the ways God comforts you. Then consider how you can be more like Him when providing comfort to a friend in need.

☩

I, EVEN I, AM HE WHO COMFORTS YOU.
WHO ARE YOU THAT YOU SHOULD BE AFRAID
OF A MAN WHO WILL DIE,
AND OF THE SON OF A MAN
WHO WILL BE MADE LIKE GRASS?

Isaiah 51:12

LIES

"I don't know what possessed me, Joe," I replied . . . sitting down in the ashes at his feet, hanging my head; "but I wish you hadn't taught me to call Knaves at cards Jacks; and I wish my boots weren't so thick nor my hands so coarse."

And then I told Joe that I felt very miserable, and that I hadn't been able to explain myself to Mrs. Joe and Pumblechook, who were so rude to me, and that there had been a beautiful young lady at Miss Havisham's who was dreadfully proud, and that she had said I was common, and that I knew I was common, and that I wished I was not common, and that the lies had come of it somehow, though I didn't know how. . . .

"There's one thing you may be sure of, Pip," said Joe, after some rumination, "namely, that lies is lies. Howsever they come, they didn't ought to come, and they come from the father of lies, and work round to the same. Don't you tell no more of 'em, Pip. That ain't the way to get out of being common, old chap. . . . Lookee here, Pip, at what is said to you by a true friend. Which this to you the true friend say. If you can't get to be oncommon through going straight, you'll never get to do it through going crooked. So don't tell no more on 'em, Pip, and live well and die happy."

—*Great Expectations*

His own insecurity caused Pip to lie. He lied to impress others, to make them think that he was something that he was not. But as Joe said, "Lies is lies. Howsever they come."

In the early church in Jerusalem, its members shared their possessions and money in a common "purse." In this way everyone had plenty. A Christian couple, Ananias and Sapphira, sold some land and secretly kept part of the proceeds for themselves. Still, they wanted everyone to think that they had given all. When Ananias brought the money to the apostle Peter, God told Peter that Ananias was lying. Peter asked him, "Why has Satan filled your heart to lie to the Holy Spirit? . . . You have not lied to men but to God" (Acts 5:3–4). John 8:44 tells us that Satan is the "father of lies" (NIV). He always lies, and there is no truth in him.

Whenever we lie, and for whatever reason, we are, in fact, lying to the Holy Spirit. We can be sure of this because God knows all things. We cannot keep secrets from Him. Ananias's and Sapphira's lies ended in death. They both dropped dead at the apostles' feet. Our lies end in spiritual death. They separate us from God the Father; however, when we strive to tell the truth, our honesty pleases God.

✠

DO NOT LIE TO ONE ANOTHER, SINCE YOU HAVE PUT
OFF THE OLD MAN WITH HIS DEEDS.

Colossians 3:9

REGARDING WORK

"But it's a dear good world, and I love it!" [said Gowen].

"It lies fair before you now," said Arthur.

"Fair as this summer river," cried the other, with enthusiasm, "and by Jove I glow with admiration of it, and with ardour to run a race in it. It's the best of old worlds! And my calling! The best of old callings, isn't it?"

"Full of interest and ambition, I conceive," said Clennam.

"And imposition," added Gowan, laughing; "we won't leave out the imposition. I hope I may not break down in that; but there, my being a disappointed man may show itself. I may not be able to face it out gravely enough. Between you and me, I think there is some danger of my being just enough soured not to be able to do that."

"To do what?" asked Clennam.

"To keep it up. To help myself in my turn, as the man before me helps himself in his, and pass the bottle of smoke. To keep up the pretence as to labour, and study, and patience, and being devoted to my art, and giving up many solitary days to it, and abandoning many pleasures for it, and living in it, and all the rest of it—in short, to pass the bottle of smoke according to rule."

"But it is well for a man to respect his own vocation, whatever it is; and to think himself bound to uphold it, and to claim for it the respect it deserves; is it not?" Arthur reasoned.

—*Little Dorrit*

In Charles Dickens's time "to pass the bottle of smoke" meant to agree to a lie. As used by Henry Gowen in this passage, it is an apathetic statement that suggests his work as an artist is meaningless. Arthur Clennam argues that respecting one's work and doing one's best is admirable, a somewhat surprising statement since Arthur is ineffectual at most everything he does.

The key to respecting whatever work God calls us to is found in Colossians 3:23. It says, "Whatever you do, work at it with all your heart, as working for the Lord, not for human masters" (NIV). And Ecclesiastes 9:10–11 adds, "Whatever your hand finds to do, do it with all your might, for in the realm of the dead, where you are going, there is neither working nor planning nor knowledge nor wisdom. . . . The race is not to the swift or the battle to the strong, nor does food come to the wise or wealth to the brilliant or favor to the learned; but time and chance happen to them all" (NIV).

We can't be certain if our work will produce the outcome we are hoping for. Some people work very little and are rewarded, and some work much and receive nothing. But if we work as if working for the Lord, then we can be content knowing that our effort is pleasing to Him.

✧

COMMIT YOUR WORKS TO THE LORD.

Proverbs 16:3

Positive Thoughts

Many a time the cloud went and came, and many a lesson it taught to Gabriel Grub, who, although his shoulders smarted with pain . . . looked on with an interest that nothing could diminish. He saw that men who worked hard, and earned their scanty bread with lives of labour, were cheerful and happy; and that to the most ignorant, the sweet face of Nature was a never-failing source of cheerfulness and joy. He saw those who had been delicately nurtured, and tenderly brought up, cheerful under privations, and superior to suffering, that would have crushed many of a rougher grain, because they bore within their own bosoms the materials of happiness, contentment, and peace. He saw that women, the tenderest and most fragile of all God's creatures, were the oftenest superior to sorrow, adversity, and distress; and he saw that it was because they bore, in their own hearts, an inexhaustible well-spring of affection and devotion. Above all, he saw that men like himself, who snarled at the mirth and cheerfulness of others, were the foulest weeds on the fair surface of the earth; and setting all the good of the world against the evil, he came to the conclusion that it was a very decent and respectable sort of world after all. No sooner had he formed it, than the cloud which had closed over the last picture, seemed to settle on his senses, and lull him to repose.

—The Pickwick Papers

It is no wonder that Gabriel Grub had a melancholy view of the world. He was a grave digger, after all, a man surrounded by life's sorrows. But when Gabriel looked around him—and in hard times—he saw people cheerful, content, and at peace. How could that be?

We have the ability to choose our attitudes. Philippians 2:5 says, "Your attitude should be the same as that of Christ Jesus" (NIV). As we read the Gospels, we see that Jesus worked hard as a rabbi and teacher of the Scriptures. Wherever He went, crowds followed Him, wanting to hear what He had to say and often asking Him for healing. Still, as exhausting as His work must have been, Jesus chose to do it without complaining. He was content to do the will of God with a positive and peaceful attitude.

Ephesians 4:22 says: "You were taught, with regard to your former way of life, to put off your old self, which is being corrupted by its deceitful desires" (NIV). Are you willing to put off your old self and put on a new attitude? You can turn negative thoughts into positive ones by believing in God's promises, found in the Bible, and by imitating the example of Jesus Christ.

✣

GOD MADE GREAT AND MARVELOUS PROMISES, SO THAT
HIS NATURE WOULD BECOME PART OF US. THEN WE
COULD ESCAPE OUR EVIL DESIRES AND THE CORRUPT
INFLUENCES OF THIS WORLD.

2 Peter 1:4 CEV

ABOUT PRAYER

"Bow to the board," said Bumble. Oliver brushed away two or three tears that were lingering in his eyes; and seeing no board but the table, fortunately bowed to that.

"What's your name, boy?" said the gentleman in the high chair.

Oliver was frightened at the sight of so many gentlemen, which made him tremble . . . These two causes made him answer in a very low and hesitating voice; whereupon a gentleman in a white waistcoat said he was a fool. . . .

"Boy," said the gentleman in the high chair, "listen to me. You know you're an orphan, I suppose?"

"What's that, sir?" inquired poor Oliver.

"The boy is a fool . . . ," said the gentleman in the white waistcoat.

"Hush!" said the gentleman who had spoken first. "You know you've got no father or mother, and that you were brought up by the parish, don't you?"

"Yes, sir," replied Oliver, weeping bitterly.

"What are you crying for?" inquired the gentleman in the white waistcoat. And to be sure it was very extraordinary. What could the boy be crying for?

"I hope you say your prayers every night," said another gentleman in a gruff voice; "and pray for the people who feed you, and take care of you—like a Christian."

"Yes, sir," stammered the boy. The gentleman who spoke last was unconsciously right. It would have been very like a Christian, and a marvellously good Christian too, if Oliver had prayed for the people who fed and took care of him. But he hadn't, because nobody had taught him.

—Oliver Twist

Proverbs 22:6 says, "Train up a child in the way he should go," but Oliver Twist had no training. He had no parents to lead the way and to provide him with a good Christian example. The poor boy did not even know how to pray.

The Lord's Prayer, found in Matthew 6:9–13, is the perfect instructional model for prayer. If we read between its lines, we discover that it includes worship, petitions, and pleas. In this simple prayer, first we worship God, our Creator, because we live under His kingship. We focus on His will and not ours. Next, we trust God to provide for our needs. Then we recognize that we all are sinners and that we can never repay God for all that He has done for us. We ask for forgiveness, and also we ask Him to help us forgive others. Finally, we ask God to protect us from evil and to make our hearts pure. The Lord's Prayer is a perfect prayer, and we can design our own prayers from its construction.

Psalm 4:3 says, "The LORD will hear when I call to Him." Prayer is God's way of allowing direct communication with Him. It is a precious gift from God, and Jesus is kind to show us how to use it.

✤

AND PRAY IN THE SPIRIT ON ALL OCCASIONS WITH ALL
KINDS OF PRAYERS AND REQUESTS.

Ephesians 6:18 NIV

MAD WORLD

"You are not to suppose that he hasn't got a longer name, if he chose to use it," said my aunt, with a loftier air. "Babley—Mr. Richard Babley—that's the gentleman's true name. . . . But don't you call him by it, whatever you do. He can't bear his name. . . . So take care, child, you don't call him anything BUT Mr. Dick."

I promised to obey, and went upstairs . . . ; thinking, as I went, that if Mr. Dick had been working at his Memorial long, at the same rate as I had seen him working at it, through the open door, when I came down, he was probably getting on very well indeed. I found him still driving at it with a long pen, and his head almost laid upon the paper. He was so intent upon it, that I had ample leisure to observe the large paper kite in a corner, the confusion of bundles of manuscript, the number of pens, and, above all, the quantity of ink (which he seemed to have . . . in half-gallon jars by the dozen) . . .

"Ha! . . ." said Mr. Dick, laying down his pen. "How does the world go? I'll tell you what," he added, in a lower tone, "I shouldn't wish it to be mentioned, but it's a"—here he beckoned to me, and put his lips close to my ear—"it's a mad world. Mad as Bedlam, boy!" said Mr. Dick, taking snuff from a round box on the table, and laughing heartily.

—David Copperfield

The French poet and novelist Victor Hugo wrote: "Strange to say, the luminous world is the invisible world; the luminous world is that which we do not see. Our eyes of flesh see only night." In *David Copperfield*, Mr. Dick viewed the world with eyes of flesh. He saw only a world that was mad.

We do live in a sinful world. The question is, how can we make our eyes see beyond the sinfulness to a world that is bright? The Bible holds the answers. First, trust that God knows what He is doing and believe that He cares for us (Isaiah 43:2). Next, follow the apostle Paul's advice, and focus on the goodness in the world (Philippians 4:8). Remember, every day, that Jesus is coming back (1 Thessalonians 4:16–17; Revelation 22:12–13) and rejoice in your salvation. Romans 10:9 promises: "If you confess with your mouth, 'Jesus is Lord,' and believe in your heart that God raised him from the dead, you will be saved" (NIV). Take heart that God's plan is to crush all evil (Romans 16:20), and God *will* win in the end.

Our world might seem mad at times, but a loving God created it, and He has not changed. As Christians, we can view the world through His eyes and see beyond the madness to its beauty, goodness, and love.

⚜

AND DO NOT BE CONFORMED TO THIS WORLD, BUT BE TRANSFORMED BY THE RENEWING OF YOUR MIND.

Romans 12:2

LAUGHTER

It was a great surprise to Scrooge . . . to hear a hearty laugh. It was a much greater surprise to Scrooge to recognise it as his own nephew's and to find himself in a bright, dry, gleaming room, with the Spirit standing smiling by his side, and looking at that same nephew with approving affability!

"Ha, ha!" laughed Scrooge's nephew. "Ha, ha, ha!"

If you should happen, by any unlikely chance, to know a man more blest in a laugh than Scrooge's nephew, all I can say is, I should like to know him too. Introduce him to me, and I'll cultivate his acquaintance. It is a fair, even-handed, noble adjustment of things, that while there is infection in disease and sorrow, there is nothing in the world so irresistibly contagious as laughter and good-humour. When Scrooge's nephew laughed in this way: holding his sides, rolling his head, and twisting his face into the most extravagant contortions: Scrooge's niece, by marriage, laughed as heartily as he. And their assembled friends being not a bit behindhand, roared out lustily.

"Ha, ha! Ha, ha, ha, ha!"

"He said that Christmas was a humbug, as I live!" cried Scrooge's nephew. "He believed it too! . . . He's a comical old fellow, . . . that's the truth: and not so pleasant as he might be. However, his offences carry their own punishment, and I have nothing to say against him."

—A Christmas Carol

In his article "The Winsome Witness," Charles Swindoll calls laughter "the most beautiful and beneficial therapy God ever granted humanity."[2] Dickens also saw the benefits of laughter. He often used irony and satire to make his readers laugh. In this scene from *A Christmas Carol*, we see the contrast between Scrooge, a grumpy, anything-but-merry old man, and his young, fun-loving nephew. Laughter was a foreign concept to Ebenezer Scrooge. He saw no value in being merry, just as he saw no value in people celebrating Christmastime.

Yet the Bible is filled with stories of rejoicing and celebration. One example is when Sarah gave birth to her son—when she was a very old woman. It was such an unbelievable miracle that Sarah laughed with joy. She said, "God has made me laugh, and all who hear will laugh with me" (Genesis 21:6).

God's own sense of humor is apparent in the story of Balaam and the talking donkey (Numbers 22). Imagine the man, Balaam, beating his poor donkey, when she opens her mouth and says, "What have I done to you, that you have struck me?" (v. 28). Surely, God must have laughed at Balaam's shock and surprise when his animal spoke to him. Proverbs 17:22 reminds us, "A cheerful heart is good medicine, but a crushed spirit dries up the bones" (NIV). So remember to laugh, long and often. It's good for you!

⚜

He will yet fill your mouth with laughing,
and your lips with rejoicing.

Job 8:21

THE BIBLE

The eyes of Alice had all this time been fixed on Harriet . . . She said now:

"I have felt . . . that I should like you to know this. It might explain, I have thought, something that used to help to harden me. . . . I somehow made it out that when ladies had bad homes and mothers, they went wrong in their way, too . . . That is all past. It is like a dream, now, which I cannot quite remember or understand. It has been more and more like a dream, every day, since you began to sit here, and to read to me. I only tell it you, as I can recollect it. Will you read to me a little more?" . . .

Harriet complied and read—read the eternal book for all the weary, and the heavy-laden; for all the wretched, fallen, and neglected of this earth—read the blessed history, in which the blind lame palsied beggar, the criminal, the woman stained with shame, the shunned of all our dainty clay, has each a portion, that no human pride, indifference, or sophistry, through all the ages that this world shall last, can take away, or by the thousandth atom of a grain reduce—read the ministry of Him who, through the round of human life, and all its hopes and griefs, from birth to death, from infancy to age, had sweet compassion for, and interest in, its every scene and stage, its every suffering and sorrow.

—Dombey and Son

In *Dombey and Son*, when Harriet Carker read the Bible to Alice Brown, Alice found a sense of knowing right from wrong. She put the past behind her and moved on in faith. Abraham Lincoln said about the Bible, "In regard to this Great book, I have but to say, it is the best gift God has given to man. All the good the Savior gave to the world was communicated through this book. But for it we could not know right from wrong. All things most desirable for man's welfare, here and hereafter, are to be found portrayed in it."

About itself, the Bible says: "All Scripture is God-breathed and is useful for teaching, rebuking, correcting and training in righteousness" (2 Timothy 3:16 NIV). "[God's] word is a lamp for my feet, a light on my path" (Psalm 119:105 NIV). "For the word of God is alive and active. . . . It judges the thoughts and attitudes of the heart" (Hebrews 4:12 NIV).

The Bible is valuable to our daily living in so many ways. It strengthens our faith, brings us back to God when we go astray, and leads unbelievers to Christ. It holds comforting words of hope and peace for difficult times. The Bible celebrates our salvation, provides words of wisdom, and gives invaluable information about the character of God through the person of Jesus Christ. It is, in truth, the light for our lives.

✣

THE GRASS WITHERS, THE FLOWER FADES, BUT THE
WORD OF OUR GOD STANDS FOREVER.

Isaiah 40:8

Regarding Change

It was, by this time, within an hour of noon, and although a dense vapour still enveloped the city they had left, as if the very breath of its busy people hung over their schemes of gain and profit, and found greater attraction there than in the quiet region above, in the open country it was clear and fair. Occasionally, in some low spots they came upon patches of mist which the sun had not yet driven from their strongholds; but these were soon passed, and as they laboured up the hills beyond, it was pleasant to look down, and see how the sluggish mass rolled heavily off, before the cheering influence of day. A broad, fine, honest sun lighted up the green pastures and dimpled water with the semblance of summer, while it left the travellers all the invigorating freshness of that early time of year. The ground seemed elastic under their feet. . . .

The day wore on, and all these bright colours subsided, and assumed a quieter tint, like young hopes softened down by time, or youthful features by degrees resolving into the calm and serenity of age. But they were scarcely less beautiful in their slow decline, than they had been in their prime; for nature gives to every time and season some beauties of its own; and from morning to night, as from the cradle to the grave, is but a succession of changes so gentle and easy, that we can scarcely mark their progress.

—*The Life and Adventures of Nicholas Nickleby*

Dickens idealized the countryside, perhaps because his city settings were often so bleak. Here, in his legendary descriptive style, the author reveals the subtleness of God's seasonal changes as Nicholas and his friend Smike walk through the landscape in springtime.

Just as God does in nature, He also changes the seasons of our lives. In Ecclesiastes 3, King Solomon wrote: "To everything there is a season, a time for every purpose under heaven: a time to be born, and a time to die; a time to plant, and a time to pluck what is planted; . . . a time to weep, and a time to laugh; a time to mourn, and a time to dance; . . . a time to embrace, and a time to refrain from embracing" (vv. 1–5).

Everything must change. Nothing stays the same. Some changes—like the seasonal changes described in Dickens's works—are expected, beautiful, and welcome. Other changes come unexpectedly, unwanted, and leave us wondering what to do. The answer for changing times is to put your faith in God, who does not change (Malachi 3:6). Solomon said that God makes "everything beautiful in its time" (Ecclesiastes 3:11). He transforms the winters of our lives into spring. When we accept the changes and ask God to make them beautiful, our faith grows and blooms like His landscapes in springtime.

⚜

WHILE THE EARTH REMAINS, SEEDTIME AND HARVEST,
COLD AND HEAT, WINTER AND SUMMER, AND DAY
AND NIGHT SHALL NOT CEASE.

Genesis 8:22

SERVICE

[Mr. Doyce] was a man of . . . good sense; . . . He was the son of a north-country blacksmith, and had originally been apprenticed . . . to a lock-maker; . . . he had "struck out a few little things" at the lock-maker's, which had led to his being released from his indentures with a present, which present had enabled him to . . . bind himself to a working engineer, under whom he had laboured hard . . . seven years. His time being out, he had "worked in the shop" . . . seven or eight years more; and he had . . . an offer to go to Lyons, . . . and from Lyons . . . to Germany . . . However, he had naturally felt a preference for his own country, and a wish to gain distinction there, and to do whatever service he could. . . . And so he had come home. . . .

"It is much to be regretted," said Clennam, "that you ever turned your thoughts that way, Mr. Doyce."

"True, sir, true to a certain extent. But what is a man to do? If he has the misfortune to strike out something serviceable to the nation, he must follow where it leads him."

"Hadn't he better let it go?" said Clennam.

"He can't do it," said Doyce, shaking his head with a thoughtful smile. "It's not put into his head to be buried. It's put into his head to be made useful. You hold your life on the condition that to the last you shall struggle hard for it."

—Little Dorrit

In Dickens's eleventh novel, *Little Dorrit*, he conveyed a sense of pessimism about the state of the world. This is reflected in the exchange between business partners Daniel Doyce and Arthur Clennam. The message in this scene is that we must follow where our abilities lead us, but a purposeful life does not come without difficulties.

The apostle Paul lived a purposeful, yet difficult, life. He went wherever he was needed to serve the Lord, always working consistently and boldly to spread the gospel of Jesus Christ. Angry mobs confronted him; he was ridiculed, imprisoned, and ultimately executed. But he never "let go" of his mission to serve. Instead of viewing his difficulties with pessimism, he faced them with a positive attitude and faith that God would see him through.

First Peter 4:10 teaches us to be good stewards of our abilities by using them to serve one another. Through our service, we glorify God and build up our brothers and sisters in Christ. First Samuel 12:24 says, "But be sure to have respect for the Lord. Serve him faithfully. Do it with all your heart. Think about the great things he has done for you" (NIRV). As you go through this day, remember Paul and—rather than seeing obstacles—try to see opportunities to serve and glorify the Lord.

☙

THEREFORE, MY BELOVED BRETHREN, BE
STEADFAST, IMMOVABLE, ALWAYS ABOUNDING IN
THE WORK OF THE LORD, KNOWING THAT YOUR
LABOR IS NOT IN VAIN IN THE LORD.

1 Corinthians 15:58

ABOUT MONEY

Young Ralph Nickleby [avoided] all those minute and intricate calcula-
tions of odd days . . . by establishing the one general rule that all sums
of principal and interest should be paid on pocket-money day . . . on
Saturday: and that whether a loan were contracted on the Monday, or
on the Friday, the amount of interest should be . . . the same. Indeed
he argued . . . that it ought to be rather more for one day than for five,
inasmuch as the borrower might in the former case be very fairly presumed
to be in great extremity, otherwise he would not borrow at all with such
odds against him. . . .

On the death of his father, Ralph Nickleby, who had been some time
before placed in a mercantile house in London, applied himself passion-
ately to his old pursuit of money-getting, in which he speedily became so
buried and absorbed, that he quite forgot his brother for many years; and
if, at times, a recollection of his old playfellow broke upon him through
the haze in which he lived—for gold conjures up a mist about a man,
more destructive of all his old senses and lulling to his feelings than the
fumes of charcoal—it brought along with it a companion thought, that
if they were intimate he would want to borrow money of him. So, Mr.
Ralph Nickleby shrugged his shoulders, and said things were better as
they were.

—The Life and Adventures of Nicholas Nickleby

Money—the lack of it and its exploitation—is a common theme in Dickens's works, perhaps because the author's father loved money, squandered it, and was thrown into a debtor's prison, leaving his family to fend for themselves. Often, Dickens wrote about misers, like Ralph Nickleby, and showed their disregard for most everything and everyone but money.

The Bible uses this illustration: When a rich man came to Jesus, asking what he must do to receive eternal life, Jesus told him to sell all his possessions and give them to the poor. The man went away sad because he did not want to part with his money. Jesus compared the man trying to part with his money to a camel trying to go through the eye of a needle (Matthew 19:16–24). Even one of Jesus' disciples succumbed to the lure of money. Judas Iscariot accepted thirty pieces of silver in exchange for turning Jesus over to those who hated Him (Matthew 26:14–16).

These stories remind us that money is at the root of all kinds of evil. Of course, it is not wrong to be wise about making and saving money. The problem comes when money is at the center of our lives. The love of money can separate us from the love of God. The Bible says, "For where your treasure is, there your heart will be also" (Matthew 6:21 NIV).

✠

HE WHO TRUSTS IN HIS RICHES WILL FALL,
BUT THE RIGHTEOUS WILL FLOURISH LIKE FOLIAGE.

Proverbs 11:28

MERCIFUL GOD

As day deepened into evening, and darkness crept into the nooks and corners of the town . . . Barnaby sat in his dungeon . . . Beside him . . . sat one in whose companionship he felt at peace. . . .

"Mother," he said . . . "how long,—how many days and nights,—shall I be kept here?"

"Not many, dear. I hope not many." . . .

She tore herself away, and in a few seconds Barnaby was alone. He stood for a long time rooted to the spot, with his face hidden in his hands; then flung himself, sobbing, on his miserable bed.

But the moon came slowly up in all her gentle glory, and the stars looked out, and through the small compass of the grated window, as through the narrow crevice of one good deed in a murky life of guilt, the face of Heaven shone bright and merciful. He raised his head; gazed upward at the quiet sky, which seemed to smile upon the earth in sadness, as if the night . . . looked down in sorrow on the sufferings and evil deeds of men; and felt its peace sink deep into his heart. He . . . caged in his narrow cell, was as much lifted up to God, while gazing on the mild light, as the freest and most favoured man in all the spacious city; and in his ill-remembered prayer, and in the fragment of the childish hymn, with which he sung and crooned himself asleep, there breathed as true a spirit as ever studied homily expressed, or old cathedral arches echoed.

—Barnaby Rudge

Dickens fashioned the prison in *Barnaby Rudge* after Newgate Prison in London, a miserable place where numerous executions took place. There, locked in a dingy cell, Barnaby Rudge found solace in God. Barnaby, a mentally challenged man, was in prison after being duped to join a group of rioters who burned Catholic churches and homes of Catholic families. Dickens's inspiration for this scene was the Gordon Riots, an anti-Catholic protest against a government proposal to reduce restrictions against Catholics in England.

The apostle Paul also spent time in a prison and found consolation in his faith in God. His crime? Preaching the gospel of Jesus Christ. Paul was not ashamed of being a prisoner, and while there he held tight to His heavenly Father and relied on Him for comfort. Like Barnaby Rudge, Paul prayed and sang praises to God (Acts 16:25).

Paul's way of dealing with his incarceration is outlined in Hebrews 4:16. It says, "Let us . . . approach the throne of grace with confidence, so that we may receive mercy and find grace to help us in our time of need" (NIV). When difficult times imprison us, we know that God is our comfort. When we cry out to Him, He will answer. "He always shows mercy to everyone who worships him" (Luke 1:50 CEV).

✢

KEEP YOURSELVES IN THE LOVE OF GOD,
LOOKING FOR THE MERCY OF OUR LORD
JESUS CHRIST UNTO ETERNAL LIFE.

Jude 1:21

CONCEIT

"I have been since," says Mr. Sapsea, with his legs stretched out, and solemnly enjoying himself with the wine and the fire . . . "a solitary mourner; I have been . . . wasting my evening conversation on the desert air. I will not say that I have reproached myself; but there have been times when I have asked myself the question: What if her husband had been nearer on a level with her? If she had not had to look up quite so high, what might the stimulating action have been upon the liver?"

Mr. Jasper says, with an appearance of having fallen into dreadfully low spirits, that he "supposes it was to be."

"We can only suppose so, sir," Mr. Sapsea coincides. . . .

Mr. Jasper murmurs assent.

"And now, Mr. Jasper," resumes the auctioneer, producing his scrap of manuscript, "Mrs. Sapsea's monument having had full time to settle and dry, let me take your opinion, as a man of taste, on the inscription I have . . . drawn out for it . . . The setting out of the lines requires to be followed with the eye, as well as the contents with the mind."

Mr. Jasper complying, . . . sees and reads as follows:

ETHELINDA, Reverential Wife of MR. THOMAS SAPSEA, AUCTIONEER, VALUER, ESTATE AGENT, &c., OF THIS CITY. Whose Knowledge of the World, Though somewhat extensive, Never brought him acquainted with A SPIRIT More capable of LOOKING UP TO HIM. STRANGER, PAUSE And ask thyself the Question, CANST THOU DO LIKEWISE? If Not, WITH A BLUSH RETIRE.

—The Mystery of Edwin Drood

Thomas Sapsea, the dull, arrogant auctioneer and mayor of Cloisterham, could not even put aside his sense of self-importance when writing the epitaph for his late wife's headstone. The words say little about her. Mostly, they are self-praise, ending with an invitation challenging the reader to equal Mr. Sapsea's eminence.

In Luke 18:10–14 Jesus says, "Two men went up to the temple to pray, one a Pharisee and the other a tax collector. The Pharisee stood by himself and prayed: 'God, I thank you that I am not like other people—robbers, evildoers, adulterers—or even like this tax collector. I fast twice a week and give a tenth of all I get.' But the tax collector stood at a distance. He would not even look up to heaven, but beat his breast and said, 'God, have mercy on me, a sinner.' I tell you that this man, rather than the other, went home justified before God. For all those who exalt themselves will be humbled, and those who humble themselves will be exalted" (NIV).

Conceit draws us away from people and more importantly away from God. Consider this: our lives are not about us or what we do to serve God, but rather about God and what He does for us.

⚜

THEREFORE HUMBLE YOURSELVES UNDER THE
MIGHTY HAND OF GOD, THAT HE MAY EXALT YOU
IN DUE TIME, CASTING ALL YOUR CARE
UPON HIM, FOR HE CARES FOR YOU.

1 Peter 5:6–7

GOD'S GARDEN

In fine weather the old gentleman is almost constantly in the garden. . . . He has always something to do there, and you will see him digging, and sweeping, and cutting, and planting, with manifest delight. In springtime, there is no end to the sowing of seeds, and sticking little bits of wood over them, with labels, which look like epitaphs to their memory; and in the evening, when the sun has gone down, the perseverance with which he lugs a great watering-pot about is perfectly astonishing . . . [His wife] is very fond of flowers as the hyacinth-glasses in the parlour-window, and geranium-pots in the little front court, testify. She takes great pride in the garden too . . . On a summer's evening, when the large watering-pot has been filled and emptied some fourteen times, and the old couple have quite exhausted themselves by trotting about, you will see them sitting happily together in the little summerhouse, enjoying the calm and peace of the twilight, and watching the shadows as they fall upon the garden, and gradually growing thicker and more sombre, obscure the tints of their gayest flowers—no bad emblem of the years that have silently rolled over their heads, deadening in their course the brightest hues of early hopes and feelings which have long since faded away. These are their only recreations, and they require no more. They have within themselves, the materials of comfort and content; and the only anxiety of each, is to die before the other.

—Sketches by Boz

ketches by Boz is a collection of Dickens's earliest short stories. The book, divided into four parts—"Our Parish," "Scenes," "Characters," and "Tales,"—describes London and its people in the early 1800s. In this passage from "Scenes: London Recreations," Dickens shows an elderly couple spending their leisure time gardening.

The book of Genesis presents another gardening scene. In chapter 2, we read that God planted a garden in Eden. He planted trees that were "pleasant to the sight" and good for bearing fruit. He put a river there to water the plants. Then He created Adam and Eve to "tend and keep" His garden (vv. 8–15). In the New Testament, Paul compared his work to a garden: "Apollos [Paul's friend] and I are merely servants who helped you to have faith. It was the Lord who made it all happen. I planted the seeds, Apollos watered them, but God made them sprout and grow. What matters isn't those who planted or watered, but God who made the plants grow. . . . Apollos and I work together for God, and you are God's garden" (1 Corinthians 3:5–7, 9 CEV).

Wherever your path may take you today, be sure to sprinkle a few seeds of faith along the way. Then watch as God's garden grows and blooms all around you.

⚜

THE LORD WILL GUIDE YOU CONTINUALLY, AND SATISFY
YOUR SOUL IN DROUGHT, AND STRENGTHEN YOUR BONES;
YOU SHALL BE LIKE A WATERED GARDEN.

Isaiah 58:11

LETTING GO

"It's in vain, Trot, to recall the past, unless it works some influence upon the present. Perhaps I might have been better friends with your poor father. Perhaps I might have been better friends with that poor child your mother, even after your sister Betsey Trotwood disappointed me. When you came to me, a little runaway boy, all dusty and way-worn, perhaps I thought so. From that time until now, Trot, you have ever been a credit to me and a pride and a pleasure. I have no other claim upon my means; at least"—here to my surprise she hesitated, and was confused—"no, I have no other claim upon my means—and you are my adopted child. Only be a loving child to me in my age, and bear with my whims and fancies; and you will do more for an old woman whose prime of life was not so happy or conciliating as it might have been, than ever that old woman did for you."

It was the first time I had heard my aunt refer to her past history. There was a magnanimity in her quiet way of doing so, and of dismissing it, which would have exalted her in my respect and affection, if anything could.

"All is agreed and understood between us, now, Trot," said my aunt, "and we need talk of this no more. Give me a kiss, and we'll go to the Commons after breakfast tomorrow."

—David Copperfield

David Copperfield, affectionately called "Trot" by his aunt, was taken aback when she spoke of her past. With the wisdom that often comes with age, David's aunt held the philosophy that it was not good to bring the past into the present unless some past lesson could aid in the here and now.

When we hold on to the past, we are not living fully in the present. The apostle Paul is a good example of a man who let go of his past as he moved forward. Paul was once known as Saul. He was an unbeliever, a persecutor of Christians. On his way to Damascus to arrest Christ's followers, Saul came to know the Lord. Later, Saul's name was changed to Paul. We don't know exactly how or why his name changed, but it created for him a new identity. It was a way of letting go of his past. When Paul thought of his past as "rubbish," he became a servant of the Lord.

God can help you let go of your past, if you are willing to believe that He is able to do it. In Isaiah 43:18–19, God says, "Forget the former things; do not dwell on the past. See, I am doing a new thing!" (NIV). Is there something from your past that is keeping you from moving fully into the present? Consider letting it go and entrusting it to God.

✣

I FOCUS ON THIS ONE THING: FORGETTING THE PAST
AND LOOKING FORWARD TO WHAT LIES AHEAD.

Philippians 3:13 NLT

DESIRES

"I am not a man to be moved by a pretty face," muttered Ralph sternly. "There is a grinning skull beneath it, and men like me who look and work below the surface see that, and not its delicate covering. And yet I almost like the girl, or should if she had been less proudly and squeamishly brought up. . . ."

Notwithstanding the deadly hatred which Ralph felt towards Nicholas, and the bitter contempt with which he sneered at poor Mrs. Nickleby—notwithstanding the baseness with which he had behaved, and was then behaving, and would behave again if his interest prompted him, towards Kate herself—still there was, strange though it may seem, something humanising and even gentle in his thoughts at that moment. He thought of what his home might be if Kate were there; he placed her in the empty chair, looked upon her, heard her speak; he felt again upon his arm the gentle pressure of the trembling hand; he strewed his costly rooms with the hundred silent tokens of feminine presence and occupation; he came back again to the cold fireside and the silent dreary splendour; and in that one glimpse of a better nature, born as it was in selfish thoughts, the rich man felt himself friendless, childless, and alone. Gold, for the instant, lost its lustre in his eyes, for there were countless treasures of the heart which it could never purchase.

—*The Life and Adventures of Nicholas Nickleby*

At the end of this scene, Ralph Nickleby, the rich, hard-hearted uncle of Nicholas and Kate Nickleby, has a brief glimpse of his need for companionship. With selfish ambition and the desire not to share his wealth with his brother's poor widow and her children, Ralph had sent them away. Now, he misses the company of his young niece and realizes that some things are worth more than money.

The Bible tells us that our worldly desires, like Ralph's desire to hoard his riches, are the opposite of that which God's Holy Spirit wants for us. Along with selfish ambition, the Bible lists other worldly desires as "sexual immorality, impurity, lustful pleasures, idolatry, sorcery, hostility, quarreling, jealousy, outbursts of anger, selfish ambition, dissension, division, envy, drunkenness, wild parties, and other sins like these" (Galatians 5:19–21 NLT). To the contrary, the Holy Spirit wants our hearts to be filled with "love, joy, peace, patience, kindness, goodness, faithfulness, gentleness, and self-control (vv. 22–23 NLT).

Though Ralph's home was filled with riches, there were countless treasures of the heart that he could not buy. Had he only been willing to share his wealth with his family, he might have been rich indeed. When we become Christians, we begin the transformation from worldliness to godliness (Romans 12:2), learning to place people and relationships before things. We strive to be as much like God as possible, surrendering our worldly desires for those of the Holy Spirit (Ephesians 4:17–24).

✠

FOR THOSE WHO LIVE ACCORDING TO THE FLESH SET THEIR
MINDS ON THE THINGS OF THE FLESH, BUT THOSE WHO LIVE
ACCORDING TO THE SPIRIT, THE THINGS OF THE SPIRIT.

Romans 8:5

PERSEVERANCE

The figure showed itself aware of me, as I advanced. It had been moving towards me, but it stood still. As I drew nearer, I saw it to be the figure of a woman . . . Then, it faltered, as if much surprised, and uttered my name, and I cried out,—

"Estella!" . . .

"I have often thought of you," said Estella.

"Have you?"

"Of late, very often. There was a long hard time when I kept far from me the remembrance of what I had thrown away when I was quite ignorant of its worth. But since my duty has not been incompatible with the admission of that remembrance, I have given it a place in my heart."

"You have always held your place in my heart," I answered.

And we were silent again until she spoke.

"I little thought," said Estella, "that I should take leave of you in taking leave of this spot. I am very glad to do so."

"Glad to part again, Estella? To me, parting is a painful thing. To me, the remembrance of our last parting has been ever mournful and painful."

"But you said to me," returned Estella, very earnestly, "'God bless you, God forgive you!' And if you could say that to me then, you will not hesitate to say that to me now,—now, when suffering has been stronger than all other teaching, and has taught me to understand what your heart used to be. I have been bent and broken, but—I hope—into a better shape.

—Great Expectations

In this passage, after many years apart, Pip runs into his first love, Estella. Over time, Estella has come to realize the worth of her love for Pip, and she wishes that she had never thrown it away. Pip discovers that Estella has suffered much in her life. Still, her attitude is such that through her suffering she has become a better person. She has persevered.

The apostle Paul is a prime example of perseverance. While preaching the gospel, he was imprisoned, beaten, stoned, and shipwrecked. Many times he went without adequate food, sleep, and clothing. Still, he pressed on. In Acts 20:22–24 we find Paul saying, "I am going to Jerusalem, not knowing what will happen to me there. I only know that in every city the Holy Spirit warns me that prison and hardships are facing me. However, I consider my life worth nothing to me, if only I may finish the race and complete the task the Lord Jesus has given me—the task of testifying to the gospel of God's grace" (NIV). Even before his suffering began, Paul had made up his mind to persevere.

The Bible says that "suffering produces perseverance; perseverance, character; and character, hope" (Romans 5:3–4 NIV). God blesses those who choose to persevere.

⚜

BLESSED IS THE MAN WHO PERSEVERES UNDER TRIAL,
BECAUSE WHEN HE HAS STOOD THE TEST, HE WILL
RECEIVE THE CROWN OF LIFE THAT GOD HAS PROMISED
TO THOSE WHO LOVE HIM.

James 1:12 NIV

REDEMPTION

"This court," said Scrooge, ". . . is where my place of occupation is, and has been for a length of time. I see the house. Let me behold what I shall be, in days to come!"

The Spirit stopped; the hand was pointed elsewhere.

"The house is yonder," Scrooge exclaimed. "Why do you point away?"

The inexorable finger underwent no change.

Scrooge hastened to the window of his office, and looked in. It was an office still, but not his. The furniture was not the same, and the figure in the chair was not himself. The Phantom pointed as before. He . . . accompanied it until they reached an iron gate. He paused to look round before entering.

A churchyard. Here, then; the wretched man whose name he had now to learn, lay underneath the ground. . . .

The Spirit stood among the graves, and pointed down to One. He advanced towards it trembling. The Phantom was exactly as it had been, but he dreaded that he saw new meaning in its solemn shape.

"Before I draw nearer to that stone to which you point," said Scrooge, "answer me one question. Are these the shadows of the things that Will be, or are they shadows of things that May be, only?"

Still the Ghost pointed downward to the grave by which it stood.

"Men's courses will foreshadow certain ends, to which, if persevered in, they must lead," said Scrooge. "But if the courses be departed from, the ends will change. Say it is thus."

—*A Christmas Carol*

A Christmas Carol is the best known and the most read of Dickens's novels. Its main character, the callous and unsympathetic Ebenezer Scrooge, is often used as a model of human redemption. The message of *A Christmas Carol* is straightforward—even pitiless men, like Scrooge, can be redeemed if they faithfully accept goodness into their hearts.

Goodness comes to us through the person of Jesus Christ. Second Corinthians 5:17 promises, "If anyone is in Christ, he is a new creation; old things have passed away; behold, all things have become new." It is Christ in whom we have redemption, the forgiveness of sins (Colossians 1:14). Everyone who puts their hopes in Him is made pure, just as Jesus is pure (1 John 3:3).

Scrooge suspected that he could change the course of his future by changing the ways he thought and lived. He understood that how we choose to live leads to particular endings, and his ending led anywhere but to heaven. Redemption means being saved from an unsavory end by the grace of God. Jesus paid the price for our sins. Through Him—and Him alone—we are redeemed. All He asks in return is that we believe and obey.

☦

FOR GOD SO LOVED THE WORLD THAT HE GAVE HIS
ONLY BEGOTTEN SON, THAT WHOEVER BELIEVES IN HIM
SHOULD NOT PERISH BUT HAVE EVERLASTING LIFE.

John 3:16

LOVE YOUR NEIGHBOR

A very different personage . . . in our parish, is one of the old lady's next-door neighbours. He is an old naval officer . . . and his bluff . . . behaviour disturbs the old lady's domestic economy, not a little. . . . He is a bit of a Jack of all trades . . . and nothing delights him better than to experimentalise on the old lady's property. One morning he got up early, and planted three or four roots of full-grown marigolds in every bed of her front garden, to the . . . astonishment of the old lady, who actually thought when she got up and looked out of the window, that it was some strange eruption which had come out in the night. Another time he took to pieces the . . . clock on the front landing, under pretence of cleaning the works, which he put together again . . . in so wonderful a manner, that the large hand has done nothing but trip up the little one ever since. Then he took to breeding silk-worms, which he would bring in two or three times a day, in little paper boxes, to show the old lady, generally dropping a worm or two at every visit. The consequence was, that . . . some . . . had already found their way to every room in the house. The old lady went to the seaside in despair, and during her absence he completely effaced the name from her brass door-plate, in his attempts to polish it with aqua-fortis.

—Sketches by Boz

One can only feel sympathy for the woman in this scene, which showcases Charles Dickens's subtle sense of humor. If you have ever had a neighbor like the old naval officer, then you can understand why the woman sought solace at the seaside. Some neighbors are hard to live with and downright difficult to love.

A teacher of the law asked Jesus which commandment was the most important. Jesus answered, "'Love the Lord your God with all your heart and with all your soul and with all your mind and with all your strength.' The second is this: 'Love your neighbor as yourself.' There is no commandment greater than these" (Mark 12:29–31 NIV).

Neighborly relationships begin by loving God. We are to love Him with total commitment and then tend our relationships through His love. This is the natural course that God has planned for us. Jesus also said, "A new command I give you: Love one another. As I have loved you, so you must love one another. By this all men will know that you are my disciples, if you love one another" (John 13:34–35 NIV). We are more likely to get along with difficult neighbors, such as Dickens's old naval officer, when we hold on to Jesus' words and put them into practice.

✤

YOU SHALL NOT TAKE VENGEANCE, NOR BEAR
ANY GRUDGE AGAINST THE CHILDREN OF YOUR
PEOPLE, BUT YOU SHALL LOVE YOUR NEIGHBOR
AS YOURSELF: I AM THE LORD.

Leviticus 19:18

HUMILITY

"There are expressions, you see, Master Copperfield—Latin words and terms . . . that are trying to a reader of my umble attainments."

"Would you like to be taught Latin?" I said briskly. "I will teach it you with pleasure, as I learn it."

"Oh, thank you, Master Copperfield," [Uriah Heep] answered, shaking his head. "I am sure it's very kind of you to make the offer, but I am much too umble to accept it."

"What nonsense, Uriah!"

"Oh, indeed you must excuse me, Master Copperfield! I am greatly obliged, and I should like it of all things, I assure you; but I am far too umble. There are people enough to tread upon me in my lowly state, without my doing outrage to their feelings by possessing learning. . . ."

"This is a day to be remembered, my Uriah, I am sure," said Mrs. Heep, making the tea, "when Master Copperfield pays us a visit."

"I said you'd think so, mother," said Uriah. . . .

I felt embarrassed by these compliments; but I was sensible, too, of being entertained as an honoured guest, and I thought Mrs. Heep an agreeable woman.

"My Uriah," said Mrs. Heep, "has looked forward to this, sir, a long while. He had his fears that our umbleness stood in the way, and I joined in them myself. Umble we are, umble we have been, umble we shall ever be," said Mrs. Heep. . . . "We know our station and are thankful in it."

—David Copperfield

This humorous, self-deprecating scene from *David Copperfield* is not representative of what the Bible means by humility. Still, many people share Uriah and Mrs. Heep's misunderstanding that being humble means behaving in an overstatedly servile way and thinking that others are good and they themselves are not.

First and foremost, humility means believing that we are nothing when compared to God. In Philippians 2:5–8, the apostle Paul says, "Your attitude should be the same as that of Christ Jesus: Who, being in very nature God, did not consider equality with God something to be grasped, but made himself nothing, taking the very nature of a servant, being made in human likeness. And being found in appearance as a man, he humbled himself and became obedient to death— even death on a cross!" (NIV).

Christian humility means yielding to God and not acting with arrogance or out of selfish ambition. By practicing this sort of humility, we can react peacefully when others confront us, face criticism with grace, apologize sincerely when needed, and be courteous in all situations. Rather than a sign of weakness, this is proof that we are gaining power and strength in Christian humility. It is when we yield to God that we truly become strong.

"AND WHOEVER EXALTS HIMSELF WILL BE HUMBLED,
AND HE WHO HUMBLES HIMSELF WILL BE EXALTED."

Matthew 23:12

On Excess

It was a numerous company—eighteen or twenty perhaps. Of these some five or six were ladies, who sat wedged together in a little phalanx by themselves. All the knives and forks were working away at a rate that was quite alarming; very few words were spoken; and everybody seemed to eat his utmost in self-defence, as if a famine were expected to set in before breakfast time to-morrow morning, and it had become high time to assert the first law of nature. The poultry, which may perhaps be considered to have formed the staple of the entertainment—for there was a turkey at the top, a pair of ducks at the bottom, and two fowls in the middle— disappeared as rapidly as if every bird had had the use of its wings, and had flown in desperation down a human throat. The oysters, stewed and pickled, leaped from their capacious reservoirs, and slid by scores into the mouths of the assembly. The sharpest pickles vanished, whole cucumbers at once, like sugar-plums, and no man winked his eye. Great heaps of indigestible matter melted away as ice before the sun. It was a solemn and an awful thing to see. Dyspeptic individuals bolted their food in wedges; feeding, not themselves, but broods of nightmares, who were continually standing at livery within them. Spare men, with lank and rigid cheeks, came out unsatisfied from the destruction of heavy dishes, and glared with watchful eyes upon the pastry.

—Life and Adventures of Martin Chuzzlewit

We know that Dickens was a master at descriptions, and this humorous scene where everyone eats in excess is no exception. We often hear the word *excess* connected to eating too much; however, it can be applied to almost anything.

In Shakespeare's play *As You Like It*, Rosalind asks, "Can one desire too much of a good thing?" According to the Bible, the answer is yes. Proverbs 25:16 says, "Eating too much honey can make you sick" (NIV). The Proverbs warn of additional problems with excess: "Too much pride causes trouble" (13:10 CEV). "Keep what you know to yourself, and you will be safe; talk too much, and you are done for" (13:3 CEV). "If you want too much and are too lazy to work, it could be fatal" (21:25 CEV). Ecclesiastes 12:12 (CEV) offers that even too much study will wear you out!

The lesson here is that, indeed, there can be too much of a good thing. Nothing is wrong with most things that give us pleasure, but they become a problem when they shift our focus from God to the world. Then we want more, need more, and will do whatever it takes to get more. There is, however, one good thing that we cannot have too much of—God Himself.

✣

WOE TO THOSE WHO JOIN HOUSE TO HOUSE;
THEY ADD FIELD TO FIELD,
TILL THERE IS NO PLACE
WHERE THEY MAY DWELL ALONE
IN THE MIDST OF THE LAND!

Isaiah 5:8

ABOUT INDIVIDUALITY

A wonderful fact to reflect upon, that every human creature is constituted to be that profound secret and mystery to every other. A solemn consideration, when I enter a great city by night, that every one of those darkly clustered houses encloses its own secret . . . that every beating heart in the hundreds of thousands of breasts there, is, in some of its imaginings, a secret to the heart nearest it! . . . No more can I turn the leaves of this dear book that I loved, and vainly hope in time to read it all. No more can I look into the depths of this unfathomable water, wherein, as momentary lights glanced into it, I have had glimpses of buried treasure and other things submerged. It was appointed that the book should shut with a spring, for ever and for ever, when I had read but a page. It was appointed that the water should be locked in an eternal frost, when the light was playing on its surface, and I stood in ignorance on the shore. . . . it is the inexorable consolidation and perpetuation of the secret that was always in that individuality, and which I shall carry in mine to my life's end. In any of the burial-places of this city through which I pass, is there a sleeper more inscrutable than its busy inhabitants are, in their innermost personality, to me, or than I am to them?

—*A Tale of Two Cities*

Dickens's words here reflect the secret nature of our individualism. None of us can know everything about another, nor can any of us know God's plans for our lives. What we do know is that there is only one God, and He knows each of us inside and out. Even before we existed in our mothers' wombs, God had a plan for us.

In Jeremiah 1:5 God says, "Before I formed you in the womb I knew you" (NIV). The psalmist David added this as he said to God: "For You formed my inward parts; . . . I am fearfully and wonderfully made; . . . My frame was not hidden from You, when I was made in secret, . . . Your eyes saw my substance, being yet unformed. And in Your book they all were written, the days fashioned for me, when as yet there were none of them" (Psalm 139:13–16). The Psalms also tell us that God desires that we be faithful to Him all of our days, and that He will teach us His wisdom in our "secret heart" (51:6 ESV).

God made each one of us unique and with an individual purpose known only to Him. He intends that we use our individuality for His glory until that day when we get to heaven and come to know the secrets of our existence. Until that day, take heart in the knowledge that you are one of God's most beautiful creations.

THEN GOD SAID, "LET US MAKE MAN IN OUR IMAGE,
ACCORDING TO OUR LIKENESS."

Genesis 1:26

JUDGING ON APPEARANCE

"Pip, dear old chap, life is made of ever so many partings welded together, as I may say, and one man's a blacksmith, and one's a whitesmith, and one's a goldsmith, and one's a coppersmith. Diwisions among such must come, and must be met as they come. If there's been any fault at all to-day, it's mine. You and me is not two figures to be together in London; nor yet anywheres else but what is private, and beknown, and understood among friends. It ain't that I am proud, but that I want to be right, as you shall never see me no more in these clothes. I'm wrong in these clothes. I'm wrong out of the forge, the kitchen, or off th' meshes. You won't find half so much fault in me if you think of me in my forge dress, with my hammer in my hand, or even my pipe. You won't find half so much fault in me if, supposing as you should ever wish to see me, you come and put your head in at the forge window and see Joe the blacksmith, there, at the old anvil, in the old burnt apron, sticking to the old work. I'm awful dull, but I hope I've beat out something nigh the rights of this at last. And so GOD bless you, dear old Pip, old chap, GOD bless you!" . . .

The fashion of his dress could no more come in its way when he spoke these words than it could come in its way in Heaven.

—*Great Expectations*

In this scene from *Great Expectations*, Pip's friend Joe, a poor blacksmith, visits Pip in London. Pip has become a fine gentleman, and somewhat full of himself, and he is embarrassed to be seen with Joe. Fate has taken them in two different directions, and Joe decides that he no longer fits into Pip's life. The final sentence here shows that Joe's genuine words have put Pip into his place, or, as Proverbs 29:23 says, "A man's pride brings him low, but a man of lowly spirit gains honor" (NIV).

How might God feel about this change in Pip and Joe's relationship? In 1 Samuel 16:7, God says to Samuel, "Do not consider his appearance . . . The LORD does not look at the things man looks at. Man looks at the outward appearance, but the LORD looks at the heart" (NIV). In John 7:24, Jesus says, "Stop judging by mere appearances, and make a right judgment" (NIV).

Joe chose to be himself, even if Pip were to judge him. He said, "It ain't that I am proud, but that I want to be right." God judges us from a position of holiness. He judges not on our appearance or prominence in society, but rather on the attitudes of our hearts. None of us has the wisdom or insight to judge others as God does—with absolute righteousness.

☩

"JUDGE NOT, THAT YOU BE NOT JUDGED."

Matthew 7:1

STRENGTH IN ADVERSITY

I had found a packet of letters awaiting me . . . and had strolled out of the village to read them while my supper was making ready. . . .

The packet was in my hand. I opened it, and read the writing of Agnes.

She was happy . . . That was all she told me of herself. The rest referred to me.

She gave me no advice; she urged no duty on me; she only told me, in her own fervent manner, what her trust in me was. She knew (she said) how such a nature as mine would turn affliction to good. She knew how trial and emotion would exalt and strengthen it. She was sure that in my every purpose I should gain a firmer and a higher tendency, through the grief I had undergone. She, who so gloried in my fame, and so looked forward to its augmentation, well knew that I would labour on. She knew that in me, sorrow could not be weakness, but must be strength. As the endurance of my childish days had done its part to make me what I was, so greater calamities would nerve me on, to be yet better than I was; and so, as they had taught me, would I teach others.

She commended me to God . . . and in her sisterly affection cherished me always, and was . . . proud of what I had done, but infinitely prouder yet of what I was reserved to do.

—David Copperfield

This scene from *David Copperfield* comes on the heels of the passing of David's wife, Dora. David thought to soothe his grief by traveling away from his home in London. While he stayed in Switzerland, David received an encouraging letter from his friend Agnes Wickfield. She complemented him on his solid character, believing in her friend's strength to overcome his sadness and turn his affliction into something good.

There are dozens of stories in the Bible of people who overcame adversity: Shadrach, Meshach, and Abednego—three men thrown into a fiery furnace for worshipping God (Daniel 3); Daniel—shut in a den with hungry lions because of his faith in God (Daniel 6:10–23); Joseph—sold into slavery by his jealous brothers (Genesis 37:12–36); Paul and Silas—jailed for preaching the good news of Jesus Christ (Acts 16:16–40). All of these men used the strength of their faith to overcome dark times in their lives. We continue to learn from them today as we read their stories in the Bible.

Adversity often results in the strengthening of our faith. Like David Copperfield, we can choose to press on through sadness, fear, or whatever obstacles stand in our way. Like the three men in the furnace, and like Daniel, Joseph, Silas, and Paul, we can put our faith in God and allow Him to fill us with the strength to endure and keep moving forward. The Lord is always faithful to those who trust in Him.

☩

BE OF GOOD COURAGE,
AND HE SHALL STRENGTHEN YOUR HEART.

Psalm 31:24

Excellent Hope

When Harriet left the house, the driver of her hired coach, taking a course that was evidently no new one to him, went in and out by bye-ways, through that part of the suburbs, until he arrived at some open ground, where there were a few quiet little old houses standing among gardens. At the garden-gate of one of these he stopped, and Harriet alighted.

Her gentle ringing at the bell was responded to by a dolorous-looking woman, of light complexion, with raised eyebrows, and head drooping on one side, who curtseyed at sight of her, and conducted her across the garden to the house.

"How is your patient, nurse, to-night?" said Harriet.

"In a poor way, Miss, I am afraid. Oh how she do remind me, sometimes, of my Uncle's Betsey Jane!" returned the woman of the light complexion, in a sort of doleful rapture.

"In what respect?" asked Harriet.

"Miss, in all respects," replied the other, "except that she's grown up, and Betsey Jane, when at death's door, was but a child."

"But you have told me she recovered," observed Harriet mildly; "so there is the more reason for hope, Mrs. Wickam."

"Ah, Miss, hope is an excellent thing for such as has the spirits to bear it!" said Mrs. Wickam, shaking her head. "My own spirits is not equal to it, but I don't owe it any grudge. I envys them that is so blest!"

"You should try to be more cheerful," remarked Harriet.

—Dombey and Son

Mrs. Wickam, a nurse to the Dombey family, had the bad habit of looking at the dark side of a situation. Here, in *Dombey and Son*, Dickens portrays her as a woman filled with hopelessness and self-pity. By contrast, her employer, Harriet Carker, encourages her to look on the bright side of things.

The apostle Paul offered similar hopeful encouragement in his letter to the Philippians. He said, "Whatever is true, whatever is noble, whatever is right, whatever is pure, whatever is lovely, whatever is admirable—if anything is excellent or praiseworthy—think about such things . . . put it into practice. And the God of peace will be with you" (Philippians 4:8–9 NIV).

Hope is about the future, about things thought of, but as yet unseen. For believers, hope lies in faith in God and His promises. "'For I know the plans I have for you,' declares the LORD, 'plans to prosper you and not to harm you, plans to give you hope and a future'" (Jeremiah 29:11 NIV). So turn your thoughts toward those things that are excellent and praiseworthy. Choose to view life as Harriet Carker did, with an attitude of hopefulness. For when you put your hope in God, your heart will abound with joy, and your soul will be filled with peace.

⚜

NOW MAY THE GOD OF HOPE FILL YOU WITH ALL JOY
AND PEACE IN BELIEVING, THAT YOU MAY ABOUND IN
HOPE BY THE POWER OF THE HOLY SPIRIT.

Romans 15:13

A Christian Home

I glanced . . . at [Mr. Jarndyce's] face. It was a . . . face, full of change and motion; and his hair was a silvered iron-grey. I took him to be nearer sixty than fifty, but he was upright, hearty, and robust. From the moment of his first speaking to us his voice had connected itself with an association in my mind that I could not define; but now, . . . [I] recalled the gentleman in the stagecoach six years ago . . . I was never so frightened in my life as when I made the discovery, for he caught my glance, and appearing to read my thoughts . . . [He] asked me what I thought of Mrs. Jellyby.

"She exerts herself very much for Africa, sir," I said.

"Nobly!" returned Mr. Jarndyce. "But you . . . think something else, I see."

"We rather thought," said I, glancing at Richard and Ada, who entreated me with their eyes to speak, "that perhaps she was a little unmindful of her home."

"Floored!" cried Mr. Jarndyce.

I was rather alarmed again.

"Well! I want to know your real thoughts, my dear. I may have sent you there on purpose."

"We thought that, perhaps," said I, hesitating, "it is right to begin with the obligations of home, sir; and that, perhaps, while those are overlooked and neglected, no other duties can possibly be substituted for them."

"The little Jellybys," said Richard, coming to my relief, "are really—I can't help expressing myself strongly, sir—in a devil of a state."

—*Bleak House*

Mrs. Jellyby—rich, charitable, and so caught up in creating settlements in Africa—neglected her family. Her husband, children, and household all suffered as she dedicated herself to helping the Africans. Mrs. Jellyby's daughter's pleas for attention fell on deaf ears, and the Jellyby children ran wild.

First Timothy 5:8 tells us that charity begins at home. It says, "Anyone who does not provide for their relatives, and especially for their own household, has denied the faith and is worse than an unbeliever" (NIV). The Bible clearly outlines the distinctive qualities of a charitable Christian home. Ephesians 5 speaks on the traits of Christian marriage (vv. 22–24), Ephesians 6 reminds children to honor their parents (vv. 1–3), and Deuteronomy 6 emphasizes that God must always be our first priority (vv. 5–9).

When God is the foundation of a Christian home, and when a family lives by the words of the Bible, then generosity and helpfulness follow. Husbands and wives act as "one flesh." Together, they create the Christian framework. Children learn obedience through Christian love and carry their moral upbringing into adulthood. When charity, in this form, begins at home, then family members can extend their charity to others by setting a good Christian example.

✣

A GOOD TREE CANNOT BEAR BAD FRUIT, NOR CAN
A BAD TREE BEAR GOOD FRUIT. EVERY TREE THAT
DOES NOT BEAR GOOD FRUIT IS CUT DOWN AND
THROWN INTO THE FIRE. THEREFORE BY THEIR
FRUITS YOU WILL KNOW THEM.

Matthew 7:18–20

FRUIT OF THE SPIRIT

Full seven happy years I have been the mistress of Bleak House. The few words that I have to add to what I have written are soon penned; then I and the unknown friend to whom I write will part for ever. Not without much dear remembrance on my side. Not without some, I hope, on his or hers. . . .

We are not rich in the bank, but we have always prospered, and we have quite enough. I never walk out with my husband but I hear the people bless him. I never go into a house of any degree but I hear his praises or see them in grateful eyes. I never lie down at night but I know that in the course of that day he has alleviated pain and soothed some fellow-creature in the time of need. I know that from the beds of those who were past recovery, thanks have often, often gone up, in the last hour, for his patient ministration. Is not this to be rich?

The people even praise me as the doctor's wife. The people even like me as I go about, and make so much of me that I am quite abashed. I owe it all to him, my love, my pride! They like me for his sake, as I do everything I do in life for his sake. . . .

"What have you been thinking about, my dear?" said Allan then. . . .

"I have been thinking that I thought it was impossible that you COULD have loved me any better."

—Bleak House

In this last chapter from *Bleak House*, Charles Dickens offers us a lesson regarding wealth. Esther Woodcourt, who likes to analyze things, reflects here on the true meaning of richness. True wealth, she decides, is not so much about money as it is sowing and reaping kindness. Her husband, Allan, is Esther's example of true prosperity. His kind, giving nature leaves everyone he meets with no reason to dislike him. They return his kindness with blessings and praise.

The Bible speaks about "the fruit of the spirit." Galatians 5:22–23 describes this "fruit" as "love, joy, peace, patience, kindness, goodness, faithfulness, gentleness and self-control" (NIV). When we practice these qualities, we reflect God's character. Second Corinthians 9:6 adds this: "Whoever sows sparingly will also reap sparingly, and whoever sows generously will also reap generously" (NIV).

Dr. Allan Woodcourt was a man who sowed generously and reaped good fruit. You can do likewise. First Timothy 6:9–11 offers this advice: "The love of money is a root of all kinds of evil. Some people, eager for money, have wandered from the faith and pierced themselves with many griefs. But you, . . . flee from all this, and pursue righteousness, godliness, faith, love, endurance and gentleness" (NIV). This is true wealth.

✣

A GOOD NAME IS TO BE CHOSEN RATHER THAN GREAT RICHES,
LOVING FAVOR RATHER THAN SILVER AND GOLD.
THE RICH AND THE POOR HAVE THIS IN COMMON,
THE LORD IS THE MAKER OF THEM ALL.

Proverbs 22:1–2

GOSSIP

Everybody said so.

Far be it from me to assert that what everybody says must be true. Everybody is, often, as likely to be wrong as right. In the general experience, everybody has been wrong so often, and it has taken, in most instances, such a weary while to find out how wrong . . .

Everybody said he looked like a haunted man. . . . He did.

Who could have seen his hollow cheek; his sunken brilliant eye; his black-attired figure, . . . his grizzled hair hanging, like tangled sea-weed, about his face . . . but might have said he looked like a haunted man?

Who could have observed his manner, taciturn, thoughtful, gloomy, . . . with a distraught air of . . . listening to some old echoes in his mind, but might have said it was the manner of a haunted man?

Who could have heard his voice, slow-speaking, deep, and grave, . . . but might have said it was the voice of a haunted man?

Who that had seen him in his inner chamber, part library and part laboratory,—for he was, as the world knew, far and wide, a learned man in chemistry . . . —who that had seen him there, upon a winter night, alone, . . . his work done, and he pondering in his chair before the rusted grate and red flame, moving his thin mouth as if in speech, but silent as the dead, would not have said that the man seemed haunted and the chamber too?

—The Haunted Man and the Ghost's Bargain

The Haunted Man and the Ghost's Bargain is the fifth and last of Charles Dickens's Christmas novellas. The story begins: "Everybody said so. . . . Everybody is, often, as likely to be wrong as right." We could exchange the word "everybody" with the name of a friend or coworker, or our own name, and the fact remains that gossip is secondhand hearsay.

What do the Scriptures say about gossip? In Exodus 20 we find the Ten Commandments, God's law for humanity. The ninth commandment says: "You shall not bear false witness against your neighbor" (v. 16). By sharing second-hand information, a gossiper risks passing along untruths. Proverbs 16:28 tells us that gossip separates close friends, and Proverbs 20:19 cautions us not to listen to gossip. Romans 1:29 calls gossip "wicked."

Gossip is everywhere in our culture. We read it in tabloids, and we hear celebrity gossip on television shows. Most of the time gossip is a distorted version of the truth. Nothing good comes from it. It destroys trust, and it is hurtful. But we can stop gossip before it begins by being watchful of what we say. When love is at the root of what comes from our mouths (Ephesians 4:29), then our words are encouraging and positive. We please the Lord when we build up His people with our words.

✛

THE WORDS OF A TALEBEARER ARE LIKE TASTY TRIFLES,
AND THEY GO DOWN INTO THE INMOST BODY.

Proverbs 18:8

KNOWING GOD

He reached the house. . . . Oliver stopped, and peeped into the garden.
A child was weeding one of the little beds. . . . He raised his pale face and
disclosed the features of one of his former companions. Oliver felt glad to
see him, before he went; for, though younger than himself, he had been his
little friend and playmate. . . .

"Hush, Dick!" said Oliver, as the boy ran to the gate, and thrust his
thin arm between the rails to greet him. . . . "You musn't say you saw me,
Dick. . . . I am running away. They beat and ill-use me, Dick; and I am
going to seek my fortune, some long way off. . . . How pale you are!"

"I heard the doctor tell them I was dying," replied the child . . . "I am
very glad to see you . . . but don't stop, don't stop!"

"Yes, yes, I will, to say good-b'ye to you," replied Oliver. "I shall see
you again, Dick. . . . You will be well and happy!"

"I hope so," replied the child. ". . . I dream so much of Heaven,
and Angels, and kind faces that I never see when I am awake. Kiss me,"
said the child, climbing up the low gate, and flinging his little arms round
Oliver's neck. "Good-b'ye, . . . ! God bless you!"

The blessing was from a young child's lips, but it was the first that
Oliver had ever heard invoked upon his head; and through the struggles
and sufferings, and troubles and changes, of his after life, he never once
forgot it.

—Oliver Twist

With love from his little friend and three powerful words, Oliver Twist began to know God. The artist Vincent van Gogh wrote in a letter to his younger brother, Theo: "I cannot help thinking that the best way of knowing God is to love many things. Love this friend, this person, this thing, whatever you like, and you will be on the right road to understanding Him better . . . But you must love with a sublime, genuine, profound sympathy, with devotion, with intelligence, and you must try all the time to understand Him more, better and yet more. That will lead to God, that will lead to an unshakeable faith."

Love for others—and by others—gives us a glimpse of God. For "love is of God; and everyone who loves is born of God and knows God" (1 John 4:7). By studying the Bible we can obtain a greater understanding of God's love, a love so great "that He gave His only begotten Son, that whoever believes in Him should not perish but have everlasting life" (John 3:16). Only through God's Son are we able to come to Him. Jesus said, "I am the way, the truth, and the life. No one comes to the Father except through Me" (14:16).

"God bless you." Just a few little words—spoken out of love to Oliver Twist by a very young friend—words that Oliver carried forever. "For God so loved the world"—just a few little words that will change your life and carry you forever as well.

&

GOD SHALL BLESS US.

Psalm 67:7

HONESTY

Tired of working, and conversing with Miss Twinkleton, [Rosa] suggested working and reading: to which Miss Twinkleton readily assented, as an admirable reader, of tried powers. But Rosa soon made the discovery that Miss Twinkleton didn't read fairly. She cut the love-scenes, interpolated passages in praise of female celibacy, and was guilty of other glaring pious frauds. As an instance in point, take the glowing passage: "Ever dearest and best adored,—said Edward, clasping the dear head to his breast, and drawing the silken hair through his caressing fingers, from which he suffered it to fall like golden rain,—ever dearest and best adored, let us fly from the unsympathetic world and the sterile coldness of the stony-hearted, to the rich warm Paradise of Trust and Love." Miss Twinkleton's fraudulent version tamely ran thus: "Ever engaged to me with the consent of our parents on both sides, and the approbation of the silver-haired rector of the district,"—said Edward, respectfully raising to his lips the taper fingers so skilful in embroidery, tambour, crochet, and other truly feminine arts,—"let me call on thy papa ere to-morrow's dawn has sunk into the west, and propose a suburban establishment, lowly it may be, but within our means, where he will be always welcome as an evening guest, and where every arrangement shall invest economy, and constant interchange of scholastic acquirements with the attributes of the ministering angel to domestic bliss."

—The Mystery of Edwin Drood

The Mystery of Edwin Drood was Charles Dickens's final work. The story, first published in monthly installments, remains a mystery on two counts. Mr. Dickens suffered a stroke after working on chapter 23, and he died the next day. In chapter 22, he left us this humorous passage in which Rosa Bud's chaperone, Miss Twinkleton, twists the truth.

Miss Twinkleton's changing the story to fit her desires may seem trivial, but the Bible says this: "Whoever can be trusted with very little can also be trusted with much, and whoever is dishonest with very little will also be dishonest with much" (Luke 16:10 NIV). It also reminds us that "truth will last forever; lies are soon found out" (Proverbs 12:19 CEV). Dishonesty, even "white lies," separates us from God: "The LORD detests lying lips, but he delights in men who are truthful" (Proverbs 12:22 NIV).

Little white lies are all around us these days as the enemy tries to lure us away from doing what is right. The problem with little white lies is that they become habitual. Before long, they roll off our tongues without us even noticing. The Bible says in John 9:24 that we give glory to God by telling the truth. As Christians, our responsibility is to become more like God, who never lies.

✠

DO NOT LIE TO ONE ANOTHER, SINCE YOU HAVE PUT
OFF THE OLD MAN WITH HIS DEEDS, AND HAVE PUT
ON THE NEW MAN WHO IS RENEWED IN KNOWLEDGE
ACCORDING TO THE IMAGE OF HIM WHO CREATED HIM.

Colossians 3:9–10

WORSHIP

A brilliant morning shines on the old city. Its antiquities and ruins are surpassingly beautiful, with a lusty ivy gleaming in the sun, and the rich trees waving in the balmy air. Changes of glorious light from moving boughs, songs of birds, scents from gardens, woods, and fields—or, rather, from the one great garden of the whole cultivated island in its yielding time—penetrate into the Cathedral, subdue its earthy odour, and preach the Resurrection and the Life. The cold stone tombs of centuries ago grow warm; and flecks of brightness dart into the sternest marble corners of the building, fluttering there like wings.

Comes Mr. Tope with his large keys, and yawningly unlocks and sets open. Come Mrs. Tope and attendant sweeping sprites. Come, in due time, organist and bellows-boy, peeping down from the red curtains in the loft, fearlessly flapping dust from books up at that remote elevation, and whisking it from stops and pedals. Come sundry rooks, from various quarters of the sky, back to the great tower; who may be presumed to enjoy vibration, and to know that bell and organ are going to give it them. Come a very small and straggling congregation indeed: chiefly from Minor Canon Corner and the Precincts. Come Mr. Crisparkle, fresh and bright; and his ministering brethren, not quite so fresh and bright. Come the Choir in a hurry (always in a hurry, and struggling into their nightgowns at the last moment, like children shirking bed).

—The Mystery of Edwin Drood

This lovely description of preparations for Sunday worship represents some of the last words ever written by Charles Dickens. A few paragraphs later, he set aside his work for the day, and that evening, at dinner, Dickens collapsed and lost consciousness. Charles Dickens died on June 9, 1870, and later, he was buried in Poet's Corner at Westminster Abbey, in London.

Dickens left behind a legacy of works that are still popular today. And many of those works reflect the moral truths found in the Bible, guiding our thoughts back to the One who created us all. As Psalm 150 says, "Praise the LORD! Praise God in His sanctuary; praise Him in His mighty firmament! Praise Him for His mighty acts; praise Him according to His excellent greatness! Praise Him with the sound of the trumpet; praise Him with the lute and harp! Praise Him with the timbrel and dance; praise Him with stringed instruments and flutes! Praise Him with loud cymbals; praise Him with clashing cymbals! Let everything that has breath praise the LORD. Praise the LORD!" For the Bible tells us: "Yet a time is coming and has now come when the true worshipers will worship the Father in the Spirit and in truth, for they are the kind of worshipers the Father seeks" (John 4:23 NIV).

The inspiration of God is evident in so many of Dickens's writings. Let it be that the inspiration of God is also so evident in your life each and every day.

✤

LET THE WORD OF CHRIST DWELL IN YOU RICHLY IN ALL
WISDOM, TEACHING AND ADMONISHING ONE ANOTHER
IN PSALMS AND HYMNS AND SPIRITUAL SONGS, SINGING
WITH GRACE IN YOUR HEARTS TO THE LORD.

Colossians 3:16

HARLES JOHN HUFFAM DICKENS was born on February 7, 1812, in Portsmouth, Hampshire, England. Several years later, he moved with his family to London, the city that would later serve as inspiration for his novels. As a child, he attended a Baptist school for boys until age eleven, when his father was sent to debtors' prison. Needing to help support his family, Charles began working ten-hour days in a factory, an experience that would later influence the repeating themes of poverty and social injustice in his works.

At age thirteen, Charles returned to school to complete his formal education, this time at London's Wellington House Academy. The quest for learning and self-education remained an important part of his life. On April 2, 1836, in St. Luke's Church, Chelsea, England, Charles Dickens married Catherine Hogarth, and together they raised ten children.

Dickens's first book was published the same year as his marriage. He soon became one of the most prolific writers of the Victorian Era and enjoyed immediate and immense popularity. He was recognized as a nineteenth-century advocate for the poor and the oppressed, and his mastery of prose allowed his characters to become remarkably real to his readers. Two hundred years after his birth, his work transcends time. His fiction and nonfiction are still widely taught today and continue to influence readers and cultures around the world.

This influence includes the Christian ideals, biblical references, and Scripture verses that were part of Dickens's faith and his writing. When his children left home, he gave each a New Testament, and in 1849 he wrote a simple book—a retelling of the Gospel narratives—called *The Life of Our Lord*. Dickens never intended to publish *The Life of Our Lord*; he wrote it to teach his children about the life and ministry of Jesus Christ and requested that it not be made public until the last of them had died. It finally was set to print eighty-five years later, in 1934.

Charles Dickens died of a stroke on June 9, 1870, while at work on his novel *The Mystery of Edwin Drood*. Although the characters and stories he gave us remain a treasured and permanent part of our culture and our literary history, his last will and testament suggests that the author's final thoughts were not of his writing but of his children and his Lord: "I commit my soul to the mercy of God through our Lord and Saviour Jesus Christ, and I exhort my dear children humbly to try to guide themselves by the teaching of the New Testament in its broad spirit, and to put no faith in any man's narrow construction of its letter here or there."

Hear my prayer, O heavenly Father,
Ere I lay me down to sleep;
Bid Thy Angels, pure and holy,
Round my bed their vigil keep . . .
None shall measure out Thy patience
By the span of human thought;
None shall bound the tender mercies
Which Thy Holy Son has bought.

—From "A Child's Hymn"

Dickens's Major Works

Sketches by Boz (1836)
Pickwick Papers (1836–37)
Oliver Twist (1837–39)
Nicholas Nickleby (1838–39)
The Old Curiosity Shop (1840–41)
Barnaby Rudge (1841)
A Christmas Carol (1843)
Martin Chuzzlewit (1843–44)
The Cricket on the Hearth (1845)
Dombey and Son (1846–48)
David Copperfield (1849–50)
Bleak House (1852–53)
Hard Times (1854)
Little Dorrit (1855–57)
A Tale of Two Cities (1859)
Great Expectations (1860–61)
Our Mutual Friend (1864–65)
The Mystery of Edwin Drood (1870, unfinished)

My meaning simply is, that whatever I have tried to do in life, I have tried with all my heart to do well; that whatever I have devoted myself to, I have devoted myself to completely; that in great aims and in small, I have always been thoroughly in earnest.

—*David Copperfield*

References

1. Oswald Chambers. *My Utmost for His Highest.* © 1935 by Dodd Mead & Co., renewed © 1963 by the Oswald Chambers Publications Assn., Ltd. (Uhrichsville, Ohio: Barbour Publishing).
2. Charles R. Swindoll, "The Winsome Witness," *Insights* (September 2003): 1–2, 4.